HOLIDAY HOPE

Remembering Loved Ones
During Special Times of the Year

Compiled by the Editors of Fairview Press

FAIRVIEW PRESS
Minneapolis

Distributed by
Compassion Books, Inc.
7036 State Hwy 80 South
Burnsville NC 28714
828-675-5909
www.compassionbooks.com

Published by Fairview Press, 2450 Riverside Avenue South, Minneapolis, MN 55454.

Library of Congress Cataloging-in-Publication Data
Holiday hope : remembering loved ones during special times of the year / compiled by the editors of Fairview Press.
          p.   cm.
ISBN 1-57749-074-6 (alk. paper)
1. Grief   2. Bereavement—Psychological aspects.   3. Holidays—Miscellanea.
4. Anniversaries—Miscellanea.   5. Birthdays—Miscellanea.   I. Fairview Press.
BF576.G7H65   1998
155.937—dc21   98-35489
                                                          CIP

First Printing: September 1998

Printed in the United States of America
02 01 00 99 98   7 6 5 4 3 2 1

Cover design: Laurie Duren
Text design: Corey Sevett
Art by R.W. Scholes ©R.W. Scholes, 1997

For a free current catalog of Fairview Press titles, call toll-free 1-800-544-8207.

CONTENTS

INTRODUCTION

THE CONCEPT FOR *Holiday Hope* originated in the Chisago Lakes area of Minnesota, just northeast of the Twin Cities, in 1991, and the program has grown rapidly thanks to strong involvement across the community. Working together, we planted a seed that has since been transplanted into five different communities.

Holiday Hope began with a telephone call. Mary Miller, grief support counselor for Grandstrand Funeral Home in Lindstrom, Minnesota, telephoned Fairview Lakes Regional Health Care (then known as Chisago Health Services) to request a meeting to discuss grief support for people in the community during the holiday season. I had just begun my position as community health outreach manager at Fairview, and this seemed like an excellent opportunity to partner with someone in the community. After our initial meeting, Mary and I decided to invite a local hospice to be a third partner in the project.

Together we planned a November event, which we called "Holiday Hope," that included an oral presentation, follow-up group support, and a closing ceremony. Community volunteers facilitated the small group sessions; hospice volunteers handled registration. We were overwhelmed when one hundred-fifty people attended the event. (Similar events usually drew at most fifty people). Even though the event lasted two hours, people stayed around to talk.

Comments from our participants confirmed that there was a great need for this kind of program in the community. We decided that this was an event worth repeating.

In 1992, attendance at the second annual Holiday Hope event rose to two hundred, even though there was an ice storm going on outside. We were surprised to find that many of the people who had attended the first event returned for the second. It seems there is no time limit on grieving.

In 1993, we decided to develop materials that participants could take home with them. We prepared a directory of local resources and other materials for helping people cope with grief during the holidays. Our attendance rose again—this time to two hundred-fifty. We had reached the limits of our facility. We had to expand.

In 1994, we brought in several new partners and sponsors, and repeated the program in five different locations. Foundation for Hospice Services provided the funding for speakers, and each community partnered with a funeral home and a church. A resource directory was prepared for each community, and other materials were provided as well. Attendance exceeded four hundred.

In response to the growing numbers of people attending Holiday Hope, we began offering ongoing grief support in the communities throughout the region. We expanded the number of sites, and also provided grief support for special needs. When a young man with a wife and two children was shot and killed at a local convenience store, the minister of a local church asked if we could provide support to the many people in the small community who were feeling the grief and loss. We sent two counselors and offered a five-week session for anyone who wanted to attend.

In 1995, attendance at the Holiday Hope event dipped, not because the program was failing, but rather because it was so successful: we were doing a much better job of meeting the needs of our grieving clients early on. Also, attendance was high in the early years because the program was serving people whose needs had not been met before. Several times, after a Holiday Hope program, people commented to me that the event had been the first time they had been able to deal directly and openly with their grief.

The following year brought what I consider to be a new beginning for the Holiday Hope program. Several local churches and funeral homes had joined with Fairview to produce a grief support series called "Growing Through Loss." The series offered speakers and support for small group activities. In 1997, the group came to us asking if they could assume responsibility for Holiday Hope. The program was our child. We had nurtured it and helped it grow, but now it was mature. It was time for us to let go. In December 1997, in a local church, Growing Through Loss held a holiday remembrance program based on Holiday Hope.

As I think of this transition, I am reminded of our closing ceremonies over the years. At the end of each event, we would bring out a Christmas tree decorated with different types of simple, inexpensive ornaments. We invited participants to take the ornaments home and place them on their trees in remembrance of the loved ones they had lost. Many people stopped to thank me for this simple ornament, saying it meant so much to have something to commemorate their loved ones with.

Some of my fondest memories are of the conversations I had with the people who attended the Holiday Hope events. I am grateful for having had the opportunity to work with others in the community to meet an abiding need. I hope that, in reading this, you too will find the help and support you need.

Betty Hestekin, R.N.
Manager, Community Health Outreach Services
Fairview Lakes Regional Health Care

R.W. SCHOLES   3/17/98

HELP FOR THE HOLIDAYS

SHAWN MAI earned his B.A. at Gustavus Adolphus College in St. Peter, Minnesota, and his Master of Divinity at Luther Seminary in St. Paul, Minnesota. An early loss of a parent and experience working in a nursing home caused him to want to learn more about the grieving process. Formerly Associate Pastor of Central Lutheran Church in Minneapolis, Minnesota, Shawn is currently a chaplain with Fairview Hospice.

THE REJOICING COMPASS   *Shawn Mai*

EVERY MORNING I do the same thing. At 5:50 AM, the coffeemaker timer clicks on and begins to brew the morning coffee. At precisely that same moment, the dog jumps on the bed and licks my face. I get out of bed. I go to the laundry room, feed the dog and the cat, let the dog out, and walk with the dog to the end of the driveway. I then look around to find where the paperboy threw the paper. I pick up the paper, go back into the house, pour a cup of coffee, and read the weather page. This is my daily ritual. It is a meaningful part of my day that I expect to always be the same. If the paper doesn't arrive, I miss it. If I happen to be out of coffee, I really miss it.

Each day of our lives has these simple rituals. They give us a sense of familiarity and comfort. They give our lives its unique direction and form. Special rituals give form to our holidays as well. The itineraries we follow, the things we eat, and the places we go, all make the way we celebrate the holidays as individual and unique as ourselves. We come to rely on these personal holiday traditions, and look forward to them from year to year.

When a loved one dies, holiday rituals are profoundly affected. The loss changes, in one way or another, all that you do during the holidays. Getting through the first holiday season without your loved one can become much like walking through a wilderness; you must learn new survival skills, and search for safety and familiarity in unknown territory.

Jane, a 49-year-old widow and mother of four, dreads December. She can't stand the thought of going downtown during the holiday season. She fears that her children are going to remember the holiday parade downtown and ask her to make their annual family trek to see it. This tradition had special meaning to her husband who died during the past year. The thought of facing this holiday event is quite daunting. The strings of lights, the festive department store windows, the street decorations recall happy holidays, but hers seem anything but happy.

Jane says that facing the holidays feels like standing on the edge of a wilderness. Spread out before her are situations that she has never had to face alone before and places where she fears to go. Her reaction may be similar to yours. Maybe, like her, you want to skip from November to January and pretend that the holiday season does not exist. Of course it is almost impossible to ignore all of the holi-day signs around us during these months. Also, if we try to do this, we compound the loss that we experience; we have lost a loved one, and now we stand to lose the holiday season, too.

What, then, can a grieving person do?

Well, if the holiday season seems like a wilderness, perhaps a compass will help us find our way. Let's take a look at some direc-tions that may help us get through the first holiday season without our loved one.

The first arrow on our compass points us toward **remembering.**

A while back I attended the funeral of a young mother who had died of cancer. The great tragedy of her death was that she had five young children, a loving husband, and everything to live for. When she died, many had trouble figuring out what to say to her family. After the funeral, as I waited for her husband, I overheard a couple speaking with him, trying to console him. They said, "The worst is behind you now. The best thing to do is to forget it all and just move on." No offense to those people, but that is bad advice.

We cannot force ourselves to forget. The first step in the grieving process is acknowledging your loss and the feelings you have about the loss. There are many different ways that you can remember your loved one and acknowledge your feelings. Here are some:

- *Light a candle in your home or hang a special ornament in honor of your loved one.*
- *Buy a gift for your loved one. Give it away to someone who would otherwise have no gift. Part of what me miss during the holidays is the giving and exchanging of love. Finding new ways to share love can be a part of healing.*
- *Give yourself the gift of emotions, and give motion to some of the emotion you feel as you remember. It may be helpful to pound a pillow or go outside and yell while you shovel snow. Find a way to express the intensity of your feelings, being careful not to hurt yourself, of course.*

The second arrow on the compass points us toward **reorienting**.

Grief is a normal and natural response to loss. When there is any kind of major change in your life, the feelings that you have about that change can be seen as a grieving process. It is important to recognize the change in your life and understand that things are not the same as they once were and never will be again. You must reorient yourself in light of the change. Think about what is coming up in the holidays and make a plan. Recognize where your loss will affect specific traditions. Ask yourself how you will deal with them. It may be helpful to have a family meeting to talk about memories of past events and anticipate the future. Here are some suggestions for things to consider when planning:

- *Should you change the time, location, or menu of traditional meals? Should you eliminate them altogether?*

> • *Would you like to attend different religious services?*
>   *Go at a different time?*
> • *Will you decorate differently? Have someone else*
>   *decorate? Not decorate at all?*

Remember, you and your family are the only judges as to what is right for you.

The third arrow on our compass points us toward **relying**.

You need to rely on others. Depression, irritability, sleepiness, boredom, restlessness, impatience, dissatisfaction are all things that push you into isolation. Do what you can to stay connected. Share your feelings about the holidays and the person you lost with others in your family. At times this may be difficult; you may meet some resistance to sharing feelings. Nevertheless, it is important to talk about your feelings, because to share grief is to take another step toward resolving grief.

Think about who you have to talk to. If family is not available to you, for whatever reason, redefine your sense of family. Turn to your close friends. You may be surprised at who is willing to listen. At the same time, do not give up if one person you expected would be a good listener disappoints you. One widower who found it tough but necessary to talk about his grief sought out a longtime neighbor, someone with whom he and his wife had shared big things in life, but she simply refused to talk about the loss. This neighbor could and would cook anything for him but she just couldn't talk or listen. That's okay. There are others whose gift is to talk and listen. Keep seeking those people out. You may be pleasantly surprised who is there.

The fourth arrow on our compass points us toward **relaxing**.

Pace yourself and take care of yourself during the holiday season. It is a good idea to plan ahead, so that you may balance the many holiday demands on your time and energy with periods of rest. Learn to say no to the demands of the season if they become overwhelming. Limit the number of parties or late nights in one week, the number of hours spent shopping, baking, or cleaning. Listen to your body; it will tell you when you are pushing too hard.

Give yourself permission to relax. Recently a friend's mother died of cancer. He found his energy level was lower, so he decided to schedule a massage for himself every other week as a way to take care of himself. The sessions helped him relax, and he found his energy level was better. You can find your own ways to relax.

In our journey through the wilderness of holiday grief, we will face dangers. Sometimes just our fear of those dangers is enough to paralyze us. We must remember that a wilderness is, by definition, a place where nature reigns, and that, as natural creatures, we are equipped with what we need to survive in the wilderness. If we choose to engage our grief, to share it with others, and take care of ourselves in the process, we can survive the wilderness and one day reach our destination. Our destinations will vary. We hope that we can achieve some resolution to our grief, but maybe during the holiday season we can even reach a place of **rejoicing**. The four points on our compass will help lead us through the hurt so that the joy of the season can return to warm our hearts.

PATRICIA ZALAZNIK is familiar with multiple aspects of death education for two reasons. First, because she is a Certified Death Educator, and, second, because she has coped with grief and loss in her own life.

Zalaznik is certified by the Association for Death Education and Counseling as a death educator, and has a master's degree in education from the University of Minnesota. She has had a career as a family life educator and has researched and taught about loss and death for twenty-five years. She currently is a doctoral student in death studies.

Pat is a workshop leader, publisher, and author who heads her own company, Abundant Resources, Inc., which provides books and presentations on understanding death and loss. Zalaznik's first book, a curriculum entitled *Dimensions of Loss & Death Education Curriculum and Resource Guide,* Third Edition, is the result of twenty years' work, begun as a master's thesis. It has been called "the best source on death education in the Library of Congress." Zalaznik's newest contribution to the field is *Stone Soups & Support Groups: Your Guide to a Nurturing Grief Support Group* (1996). She has also published the *Bibliography on Grief: Your Guide to the Right Resources to Cope with Loss and Death* (1995).

Pat volunteers for hospice programs. She helps facilitate grief groups at North Memorial Hospice and is a founder and secretary of the board of Déva House, the first independent children's respite hospice in the United States.

Since childhood she has experienced many death and grief issues, including several attempted suicides by her mother, her father's terminal illness, and the death of her seventeen-year-old son from cancer.

SURVIVING THE HOLIDAYS   *Patricia H. Zalaznik*

YOU ARE FACING YOUR FIRST holiday season without your loved one. Well before the holidays, you begin to ask, "How on earth can I survive, much less celebrate the holidays this year?" It is a difficult time, so be gentle with yourself and those around you who have also been affected by the loss.

The following are some suggestions of ways to help you take care of yourself during this stressful time.

PLAN AHEAD. The holidays this year will not be what they used to be, but you will endure them better if you do some advance planning and have some coping skills at your fingertips. Others may not understand your pain, but you can practice supporting yourself and each other. Think about attending a workshop on coping. It will help to share your feelings and spend time with others who have had a loved one die. You can learn from others what worked for them when they had to cope with grief during the holidays.

INVOLVE YOUR FAMILY. Just as each relationship is unique, so, too, is each person's grief when that relationship is broken by death. In a family with a surviving spouse and three children, there will be four different versions of grief. Planning for the holidays with family members may require compromise, but the result will be a holiday that meets the needs of everyone in the family. Children and adolescents will need extra support. Sometimes they are overlooked during grief, and need to be reassured and included. When you work things through together with your children, you model effective skills for them to use the rest of their lives.

COMMUNICATE YOUR PLANS. Tell your family and friends what you need and want, what you can and cannot do, what you would appreciate help with. Share the responsibilities with others. If friends ask how they may help, invite them to assist you with holiday preparations. You might even hire help.

DO IT A NEW WAY. Decide on a new way to spend the holidays. If a huge sit-down dinner seems overwhelming, you could serve one buffet style, or you could eat out. One family I knew traveled to Florida for vacation and had a Christmas picnic on the beach. Consider going somewhere, such as a dinner play or a hotel, where a part of the holiday is planned and carried out for you.

BE FLEXIBLE. If Plan A doesn't work, have a Plan B available. Remember, you are not making a commitment to doing something this way for the rest of your life; you are working your way through a challenging time. Some strategies will feel more appropriate than others.

REMEMBER YOUR LOVED ONE. Set aside special time to devote to the memory of the deceased. Have an afternoon or evening when you really focus on that person and share memories. Light candles and set out pictures. How about going through old picture albums or creating new ones? People are thinking of the deceased person anyway, so acknowledging and allowing the expression of feelings can be healthy. You might plant a tree somewhere as a living memorial. When you take the freedom to express your sadness, you may also discover some small joys.

MAKE SHOPPING EASIER. Advertising during the holidays is designed to whip you up into a shopping frenzy. Pay no attention, and do what you feel you can handle. Before you go into the stores,

organize a shopping plan. Don't waste energy guessing what to buy
for people; ask them what they want or need. Take someone along
to help, and take breaks when you need them. Consider shopping
in one place as much as possible. A favorite bookstore is a good
place to obtain a wide variety of gifts. You could shop by mail or
give gift certificates. Other good gifts are magazine subscriptions,
CDs, or tapes. Have things gift-wrapped by the store.

MAKE GREETING CARDS EASIER. Send, send a modified ver-
sion, or don't send at all; it is up to you and your energy level. Some
people who send you cards may not be aware of your bereavement,
so you could plan how to inform them. You might consider writing
a standard letter, having it copied, and sending it out. Use stickers
for return addresses and purchase printed thank you cards so you
don't have to spend your energy creating messages for them.

PREPARE FOR TOUGH QUESTIONS. Think in advance of replies
to the daunting questions such as "How are you doing?" It will
probably be asked by well-intentioned people, but will be troubling
or awkward to answer. Maybe a truthful reply like, "Sometimes
okay, and sometimes not too good," will suffice. By giving an honest response, you help teach others about grief.

SIMPLIFY THE BIG MEALS. If you are going to prepare holiday
meals, don't be ashamed to use shortcuts and disposable table settings. Take advantage of deli or frozen foods. Restaurants and grocery stores now prepare holiday meals for take out. Don't turn
down offers of help. Ask each participant to prepare or bring one
part of a meal. Ask some folks to come early to set up and some to
stay late to help with the cleanup. For yourself, try to eat healthy
foods and avoid alcohol and caffeine. How about trying non-caf-
feine spiced tea or a hot cider?

MAKE GATHERINGS EASIER. It is probably better to try to attend rather than avoid them. However, you may feel more comfortable if you have an escape plan ready in case you find yourself feeling really uncomfortable. Also, you may feel better if you go with someone rather than going alone. Give yourself permission to leave if the gathering really causes you distress. There are no brownie points for enduring an unnecessary challenge. If you feel you may be vulnerable at church, consider sitting near the back or at the end of a pew so you can easily slip out.

TAKE TIME OFF. Rest and relaxation are vital. Holidays usually add stress to our lives, and during the time of grief, this stress is increased. Spending emotional energy can be more draining than doing heavy physical tasks. Therefore, plan for rests, naps, and break times.

FREE YOUR EMOTIONS. Don't be afraid to give yourself the gift of tears. Also, remember that laughter and tears are two sides of the same coin. You may not feel like laughing as much as usual, but like tears, laughter can be a healthy release. Give yourself permission to have authentic feelings and appropriately express them. If you are feeling really depressed or scared, consider talking to a helper such as a bereavement counselor or a therapist. People who seek help will do better than people who withdraw or avoid confronting the challenges of the holidays.

TEND TO YOUR SPIRIT. At the beginning and end of each day, and in the hard moments, plan some time for prayer, meditation, and reflection. Some spiritual time can renew as well as help put things in perspective, whatever your spiritual tradition.

EXERCISE. Whatever your exercise of choice, it will be good for your spirits as well as your body to keep it up during the holidays. Exercise helps alleviate feelings of depression. Having a partner or buddy for regular exercise will make it easier.

KEEP A JOURNAL. Many intense feelings will surface for you during this season. Writing in a journal will provide you with a place to put all your feelings. Alternately, you might consider finding a phone friend, one who is in the same boat as you, who is willing to share listening time and support with you.

REWARD YOURSELF. Plan a reward for yourself after negotiating your way through an important day. This could be a simple reward such as breakfast in bed or a movie, or it could be a more substantive reward such as a massage or an expensive meal, or it could even be an active reward like swimming or skiing. Only you know what rewards you best.

THINK ABOUT NEXT YEAR. Navigating the holiday season without your loved one is usually the most difficult the first year. After this holiday season, you can decide what helped you and what you wish to change in subsequent years. In any event, it will always help to plan ahead and be gentle with yourself.

KAY JOHNSON, LSW, has worked in the hospice field for over nine years as Social Worker, Director of Volunteers, and Director of Bereavement. She currently works for HealthPartners Hospice of the Lakes in Minneapolis, Minnesota, as the Bereavement Coordinator. Kay holds a Bachelor of Science degree in Human Development and Family Studies with an emphasis in Adulthood and Aging and a concentration in Death, Dying, and Grief from Colorado State University, and is a licensed Social Worker. She has presented many workshops on loss and grief to healthcare professionals, volunteers, lay ministers, and grieving individuals. Kay has also facilitated many grief groups for survivors during her hospice experience. Kay has served on the board of the Minnesota Coalition for Death Education and Support since 1995. The insights offered in the following piece come from her years of work with survivors of loss— or those she calls "the true Grief Experts."

GRIEF AND THE HOLIDAYS

Kay Johnson

FOR BEREAVED PEOPLE, the holiday season can be a difficult time. The pain felt on these special days is an intensification of the pain felt every day. The holidays remind us of our losses and the empty space in our hearts.

Here are some suggestions of ways for bereaved people to take care of themselves when holidays approach.

REFLECTION. See yourself. Look at who you are, your needs, your feelings, your wishes, your hopes, and the possibility of one or two dreams ahead. Bereavement is about loss and healing; the goal of grief is to help you find the will to do what is best for you.

TIME. No one has enough. For the bereaved, there is never enough time. It is stripped away from us by people who, in their discomfort with our pain, try to hurry us along, and who try to fix us with platitudes like, "You should be over this by now." Take back the control you need to do what is best for you.

MEANING. Losses of any kind (not just the death of someone close) force us to explore what life means to us. We are continually reminded that life is a mystery, that fairness is rare, and that we are left with riddles and unanswered questions.

SOME HELPFUL HINTS FOR COPING WITH GRIEF DURING THE HOLIDAYS

THINK ABOUT THE HOLIDAYS AND PLAN AHEAD. Remember that your energy level and motivation are lower. Think about what you want from the holidays and what you want to do. Changing traditions can be an option, remembering that the change does not have to be a permanent one. Include other family members in your planning. Delegation, negotiation, and respect are helpful.

LISTEN TO AND TRUST YOURSELF. We are all impacted differently by a loss, so our grief and needs during this time are unique. Trust yourself.

REMEMBER THAT THE ANTICIPATION OF THE DAY MAY BE WORSE THAN THE ACTUAL DAY. Be gentle with yourself.

BE AWARE OF YOUR EXPECTATIONS OF YOURSELF AND THOSE OTHERS HAVE OF YOU. Try to make those expectations more realistic.

FIND WAYS TO HONOR AND CONNECT WITH THE PERSON WHO HAS DIED.
- Light a candle in celebration of a life and love shared.
- Give a donation in memory of the person who has died.
- Remember the gifts that person gave to you, like laughter, security, love, companionship.

DO NOT STOP THE CELEBRATION ALTOGETHER. Although we may feel like hiding out and not participating during the holiday time, this will not erase our pain. The potential for support could be taken away by not participating.

R.W. SCHOLES   1/28/98

CHAPLAIN EDWARD HOLLAND currently serves as the Coordinator of Spiritual Care and Grief Support at Methodist Hospital Hospice HealthSystem Minnesota in Minneapolis, a program he helped to start in 1979. Ed is a United Methodist minister, a board-certified chaplain, a certified Gestalt therapist, and a licensed marriage and family therapist. He is also a past president of the Minnesota Hospice Organization and currently serves as a member of MHO's Ethics Committee. Ed lives in Shoreview, Minnesota, with his wife Mary Ann, who is a music specialist with the St. Paul Public Schools. They are proud to be owned by their cat, Amber.

SURVIVING THE HOLIDAY BLUES: STOP, SIMPLIFY, AND SUPPORT

Ed Holland

IT WAS A PHONE CALL I dreaded having to make. I had tried calling several times earlier. No answer. I was in Phoenix attending an educational conference in early November. My parents were back home in Minneapolis. Early that morning my dad had undergone a colonoscopy. He hadn't been feeling well for about six months or so but had been reluctant to visit the doctor, fearing that the news would be bad. When he finally saw the doctor, diagnostic tests were ordered. Today we would know.

The "busyness" of the conference activities kept my mind elsewhere since my arrival in Phoenix the day before, but concern for my dad and mom would still invade my thoughts, despite the many distractions. I wondered how they would manage if the news was bad. How would we as a family adapt? Would my sister and brother be able to help? How would my mom manage, with her sight failing as it was, without my dad's help? What kind of patient would my dad be? How would my siblings and I be as caregivers?

In a crisis, I tend to imagine the worst case scenario and then work back from there. I prepare for the worst but pray for the best. Unfortunately, my ministry as a hospice chaplain tends to reinforce this tendency; in over eighteen years of healthcare ministry, I've seen many worst case scenarios come true. It seems a fortunate coincidence that I was attending a hospice conference at the time, because I was among empathetic and compassionate friends. A community of support surrounded me even though I was far away from home.

It was time to try calling again. As usual, Dad answered. He sounded remarkably upbeat. Maybe it was good news. "Well, it's cancer. Colorectal cancer. I'm scheduled for surgery next week, just before Thanksgiving. I guess the holidays will be a little different this year!" Prepare for the worst.

The weeks that followed were a blur, and still are now over two years later. I returned home early the next day to help my parents navigate our local healthcare maze. The surgery went well. From all indications, the cancer had not spread. Chemotherapy and radiation followed about a month later. After about two weeks, with his physician's support, Dad decided to discontinue these treatments, because, he said, "they're making me sicker than I ever felt with the cancer!" The next few months of recovery were pretty rough, but by spring Dad was feeling good again, "better than I've felt for months!" It has been over two years and, for now, no sign of cancer. Hope for the best.

A health crisis brings with it many changes, not only for the person who is ill, but for everyone who cares about that person. One of my dad's greatest concerns was that his illness would ruin everyone's holidays. That year he spent Thanksgiving in the hospital, unable to eat solid foods. He still craved the traditional meal, so we had our Thanksgiving meal at Christmas when he was better able to enjoy the traditional feast. This was just days before his chemotherapy and radiation treatments were to begin. Yes, the holidays were different for every member of the family. But ruined? No.

Holidays and other special days can be especially difficult for grieving persons and families. Often holidays serve as a painful reminder of what once was but will never be again. At these times, the past seems intensified, memories tend to be distorted as we selectively remember happier times, and our loneliness is heightened through the countless reminders of togetherness. The secular Christmas holiday has become the season of exuberance at every level. Grief, however, is in stark contrast to the season of joy. In our grief we may feel out of sync with the world around us. This dissonance has been called the "holiday blues." We must remember that when we are grieving, especially around holidays and special days, it is rational and healthy for us to feel blue. We must feel free to do what is necessary to take care of ourselves during this time.

The health crisis in my family forced us to do at least three of the things I counsel clients to do, especially when living with grief through holidays and other special days throughout the year: **Stop, Simplify, Support.**

STOP. A crisis, by its very nature, forces us to stop our routines and modify our plans. Whether it is a health crisis, the death of someone we love, or countless other kinds of losses, these experiences force us to stop, examine our priorities, and make changes appropriate to our circumstances. When I learned about my dad's diagnosis, business as usual stopped for me. The educational conference in sunny Phoenix had little meaning. My heart was many miles away with my parents back home. That was where I needed to be.

The author and lecturer, Thomas Moore, says that the greatest barrier to spiritual growth in our culture is our inability or unwillingness to stop our individual and collective "busyness" and take time for reflection. A first step in spiritual growth, then, is to break out of our overly busy routines. A life crisis forces us to stop. If we don't stop – if we try to continue business as usual – we won't be able to hear the voice of wisdom within each of us. If we do stop and listen to that voice, healing and growth can follow.

A simple way to help yourself stop in the midst of a crisis or in the hyperactivity of the holidays is to focus your breathing. Four or five slow, deep breaths can help you to stop, center yourself, and thoughtfully act rather than react.

SIMPLIFY. Even before Dad's illness, we, as individuals and as a family, had been gradually trying to simplify our holiday traditions and routines. For example, some years ago my wife and I began to limit the number of holiday gatherings we attended. Instead, we have intentionally tried to spend more time at home together. We experimented with sending Christmas letters or cards every other year and then only to friends and family members whom we seldom had a chance to visit. We put limits on our gift-giving to family members and friends, and instead donated money to our favorite charities in honor of or in memory of loved ones. Most important-ly, we have tried to use the holidays as a time for spiritual reflection, growth, and renewal.

The reality is that, in grief, you may not have the physical, emotional, and spiritual energy required to continue complicated holiday routines and traditions. Give yourself and your loved ones permission to make changes, to simplify things. Less can be more.

Simplifying your life during holidays may sound simple, but it is not easy. Some planning is necessary, even though you may not have the energy.

SUPPORT. In a crisis, emotional, spiritual, and practical support can help make the crisis more manageable. Support cannot take away the winds of change or the pain of grief, but it certainly can help us weather the storm. When we learned about my dad's cancer, our family was touched and, at times, overwhelmed by the support offered and given by family members, friends, and colleagues.

Support takes many forms, depending upon your circumstances, need, and openness to receiving and giving. What is helpful for one person may not be at all helpful for another. What is helpful now may not be helpful later. For example, my dad has always been very gregarious. This quality served him well in his career as a pharmaceutical sales representative, but in the wake of his surgery, treatments and recovery, Dad tended to withdraw. He didn't want phone calls or visitors at home, preferring, instead, to be alone, to rest. While understandable, this change worried us. Was Dad feeling sorry for himself? Was he slipping into depression? Shouldn't we do something? Gradually, however, as Dad began to feel better, he emerged from his healing cocoon, and once again accepted calls and visitors. As a family, one of our greatest challenges was learning to support Dad's desire to reject support, to be alone, until he was ready to accept all of the well-intended help that was offered.

MY DAD'S STORY illustrates the difference between inner and outer support resources. Both are important to the healing process. The inner work of grief is done at the spiritual, emotional, and cognitive levels. Withdrawing to lick our wounds is a natural part of the healing journey. During this time we can begin to rediscover, redefine, and recreate ourselves and our lives in the wake of loss and change.

The inner work of grief can be supported and facilitated in many ways, including meditation, prayer, journaling, contemplative reading, and music. A support group or conversation with a trusted, empathetic person who can comfort, guide, and sustain you on your healing journey might also be helpful. For me, weekly sessions with a psychologist who has served as my therapist and spiritual guide for many years were especially helpful as I dealt with the ups and downs of my dad's illness and recovery.

The inner work of grief is hard work, indeed. There are times when this work can drain us of the energy we need to maintain the physical and social dimensions of our lives. As cruel and unfair as it may feel, many aspects of our day-to-day life must go on, even when we are grieving. Here we must turn to our outer support resources. Practical support offered by family members and friends can be especially helpful in managing the many activities necessary to continue our daily life. Accept the offers of food, transportation, chore services, and companionship. If the offers are not forthcoming, then ask for what you need. The people who care about you want to be helpful. So practice becoming a gracious recipient. Paradoxically, accepting the gift of support from others is a gift you can give them.

When you are ready, you might want to try reaching out to support others in need. Volunteer work has been an important part of my dad's healing process. In becoming a companion to others who are hurting, you can break out of your prison of isolation, loneliness, and fear, and gradually discover a measure of comfort and peace in your grief. There are many religious and social service agencies that would be grateful for your help, especially around holiday times.

Living with the losses that come with change and the grief that naturally follows is stressful. It can take a toll on the body as well as the mind and spirit. Because of this reality, the outer work of grief includes taking care of your body through good nutrition and exercise. Eat a balanced diet. Avoid caffeine, sugar, fatty foods, and alcohol. Moderate exercise, something as simple as brisk walking for at least a half hour every other day, has been shown to stimulate the body's natural pain relievers. Additionally, there is growing evidence that moderate exercise can help combat and lift some forms of depression. You may also want to consider therapeutic massage and other forms of complementary body work designed to facilitate relaxation. Caring for your body will help you support yourself as you continue the very strenuous inner work of grief.

Each of us must take our own unique journey of grief when we experience change and loss. The journey will be filled with many surprises, dangers, and opportunities as we experience the pain of grief. Any attempts to delay or avoid the journey will only result in more pain. Although there are no shortcuts, there are sign posts that can help us along our way. We have explored three of them: Stop, Simplify, and Support. May they help you find your way on your healing journey.

ELIZABETH LEVANG holds a doctorate in Human and Organizational Systems from The Fielding Institute in Santa Barbara, California. She has conducted educational programs and lectures on grief, has led support groups, and is a consultant, speaker, and writer in the fields of human development and psychology. Recently, her work has extended to helping organizations assist grieving employees. Her deep understanding of bereavement, from both academic and personal standpoints, inspired her to author *Remembering with Love: Messages of Hope for the First Year of Grieving and Beyond* and, more recently, *When Men Grieve: Why Men Grieve Differently and How You Can Help.*

Elizabeth lives with her husband, Curtis, and daughter, Natalie, in Orono, Minnesota.

COPING WITH GRIEF
DURING THE HOLIDAYS   *Elizabeth Levang*

THE HOLIDAY SEASON calls up wistful memories and returns us to faraway places, to scenes filled with the scents and sounds of warmth and happiness. No other time of year evokes such strong images of family togetherness. For all its nostalgia and sentimentalism however, the holiday season is a difficult and often debilitating period for those of us who are bereaved. More than anything, the holidays seem to accentuate what others have and we have lost. A time of year that once was joyous and momentous now often becomes almost unbearable. Thanksgiving, Christmas, Hanukkah, and New Year's are days to endure rather than enjoy. A friend whose seventeen-year-old son died in a car accident once confided, "I'd like to rip December 25th off my calendar forever."

Those of us with loved ones who have died experience a special pain or burden during the holidays. Our lives have been altered, and our family togetherness has been disturbed forever. Trying to reconcile our reality with the idealized picture of the holidays projected by the media causes even more emotional pain. The expectations put on the bereaved, both socially and emotionally, can feel overwhelming. We may have parties to attend, gifts to purchase, and a tree to be bought and trimmed. We are expected to get in the spirit and join in the festivities just like everyone else, yet in our hearts is a gnawing pain and the constant fear that we won't make it.

A close friend once remarked how much she had come to hate Thanksgiving. "The family focus hurts me," she said. "I feel somehow out of place. It's a depressing and lonely time for me. Both my parents are dead and I don't really feel like I have much to give thanks about." Comparing ourselves to others, isolating ourselves, feeling jealous, lonely, depressed, or angry are some of the reactions that we may experience during the holiday season. Many of us also feel guilt from time to time, or are totally overwhelmed with sorrow. The holidays often take a serious toll on our self-esteem.

Still, there are ways to survive the holidays, and with a change in attitude and a bit of planning, they can become tolerable, and even enjoyable.

How can we better handle our grief during the holidays?

First, we need to acknowledge our pain. We miss our loved one. It is agonizing not to be able to spend this joyous time with him or her. We must feel free to share our pain with friends and family. By acknowledging and sharing our feelings, we allow others to support and care for us. Rather than pushing our feelings down and hoping they will stay hidden, we need an opportunity to resolve them. Only by letting the hurt out will we make room for healing.

Second, we must take charge of our lives and not leave things to chance. This does not mean putting ourselves on a rigid schedule, but rather deciding in advance what we would like to do and with whom. By taking charge, we give ourselves things to look forward to rather than things to dread. Occupying ourselves lends a purpose to our days and keeps us from feeling sorry for ourselves.

Third, we need to think more realistically and positively. What we think has a dramatic effect on how we feel. When we form positive yet realistic expectations for the holidays and accept our own limitations, we reduce the tensions and pressure we face. At the same time, we also create a little more room to breathe.

Now, how do we put these three new attitudes into practice? Here are a number of specific coping strategies:

BE HONEST. Your feelings are legitimate. We can trust that we know what is best for ourselves. If a gathering of family or friends is too painful, we can make our apologies and leave.

ACCEPT AND SEEK SUPPORT. We can let our family and friends know how they can be of assistance. If hanging ornaments on the tree feels overwhelming, we can ask a friend to lend a hand. If neighbors offer to bake cookies or wrap gifts, we can graciously accept their help and good intentions.

BE KIND TO YOURSELF. We can look for ways to nurture and care for ourselves throughout the holidays. Perhaps we will buy ourselves a special gift, sign up for a massage, or do that something we've always wanted to do. And at the very least, we can treat ourselves to an occasional smile.

HAVE A PLAN. Talking with friends and family about what we want and don't want to do during the holidays can be very helpful. Being prepared lessens anxiety.

ALTER TRADITIONS. Since circumstances have changed, old traditions may need replacing. Even simple changes, like serving another dish instead of turkey or opening gifts later in the day, may make us more comfortable.

START A NEW TRADITION. We can start afresh by adding one new tradition each year. Attending a seasonal play, decorating a special tree outdoors, or reciting a favorite poem before opening gifts are some examples.

SHOP EARLY. Avoid the holiday atmosphere by completing shopping early. We can rely on catalogs or the telephone, or enlist the aid of a supportive friend.

DECREASE YOUR COMMITMENTS. Grief saps energy, so we may need to pare down our commitments. We might consider buying instead of baking cookies, cutting down on the number of cards we send, or possibly having an artificial rather than a fresh tree.

CHERISH YOUR MEMORIES. Religious services, Christmas concerts, or other holiday events can trigger memories of our loved one. While some may be painful, memories need to be cherished, for they are an enduring and intimate connection to our loved one.

GIVE TRIBUTE. The holidays may be a special time to honor our loved one. Donating money to a special cause, offering to help someone in need, or volunteering our time and talents to a local charity are some ways to do this.

BE HOPEFUL. The pain and stress of the holidays is very real. Still, with some trial and error, things will get better. In time we will add new traditions and new memories to accommodate our changed situation.

REMEMBER THEIR LIFE. More than anything else at this time of year, we may feel a strong need to know that our loved one has not been forgotten. Setting a plate at the table for them, hanging their stocking on the mantle, or retelling stories of them are just a few ways to reassure ourselves that the spirit of this special person lives on.

RW SCHOLES   4/16/98

RICHARD J. OBERSHAW is the founder, director, and full-time psychotherapist at the Grief Center and Burnsville Counseling Clinic in Burnsville, Minnesota. He lectures nationally and internationally to professional, corporate, and lay groups on various social and psychological topics. He has authored several publications, including *Cry Until You Laugh: Comforting Guidance for Coping with Grief,* and *Death, Dying, Grief and Funerals,* as well as several audio and video tapes.

Dick has earned degrees in psychology and social work at the University of Wisconsin, LaCrosse, a mortuary science degree from the Wisconsin Institute of Mortuary Science, Milwaukee, and a master's degree in social work at the University of Minnesota. He is a wounded Vietnam veteran, private pilot, and father of two sons. He describes himself as a "serious humorist" who feels we must laugh in order to learn.

GRIEF AND HOLIDAYS
Richard J. Obershaw

PEOPLE WHO ARE GRIEVING fear holidays. Holidays can be times when they have to face more than their wounded emotions can bear. Why is grief more acute during the holidays? What follows are ten reasons why holidays can make grief more painful. None of these reasons alone may cause undue pressure, but two or three together can be enough to overwhelm a grieving person.

REGRESSION. Holiday celebrations commemorate the past. Those who celebrate mark and remember past events. Some events may be from our lifetime, some may be hundreds or thousands of years old. We send cards with pictures of a child in a manger, of a man on a cross. We light a menorah or an evergreen tree. We eat a meal in remembrance of shared feast between Indians and Pilgrims, or in remembrance of a journey out of bondage. We remember the accomplishments of a martyred civil rights leader, of great American presidents. We salute a tattered American flag, watch fireworks, or place a wreath on a veteran's grave. All of these practices and traditions cause us to look back, to regress in our thoughts to an earlier time.

Grief, too, is a regressive event. It can cause people to regress psychologically. Grieving children will often regress to more child-like behaviors, such as thumb-sucking, bed-wetting, and baby talk. Adults may find comfort in being held, rocked, or patted by those offering sympathy. In severe grief, adults may even curl into a fetal position, a sign of ultimate regression. In a more general sense of regression, grief can force us to focus on the past rather than dealing with the present or preparing for the future. Grieving adults fear the future because they are uncertain what lies ahead; thus, they go back and think about their life before it changed, when things seemed safer. The past seems safer than the future simply because we know we have survived it. The future can be a terrifying unknown.

When holiday remembrance and grief-related regression are combined, as they are during holidays, they can quickly spiral the bereaved down to new depths of grief, particularly if the holidays come soon after the loss.

SELF-CENTEREDNESS IN A TIME OF SELFLESSNESS. The holidays are a time to express our gratitude for what has been given to us, or sacrificed for us, to make our lives better. And they are a time to give to others. Solicitations from charities abound during the holidays. Gifts are purchased and exchanged, food is given to others, volunteers feed the homeless, bell ringers remind us to drop money in the kettle for the less fortunate. For most of us, it feels good to give—but not for the bereaved.

Grief is selfish. The bereaved say "I have lost, and I hurt; I am lonely and confused. I need to get to know me again. I need to be comforted. I am angry. I am sad. I. I. I." When we lose someone, we focus on ourselves—we tend to look inward rather than outward. The work of grieving is the work of re-identifying the self; thus, the bereaved are very self-centered.

The bereaved's self-centeredness collides with the holiday message of selflessness, which creates confusion and guilt. The bereaved often feel there is something wrong with them, because prior to their loss, they always felt good about giving during the holidays. Now they feel bad because they are unable to summon up the giving spirit. The loss of holiday spirit becomes yet another loss for the bereaved to cope with, making their grief even more painful.

FAMILY REUNIONS. Holidays bring families together to celebrate according to the family's traditions. The support that a family gives to the bereaved can be of great solace. So, too, the lack of support from a family can be a source of added pain for the bereaved. People move through the grieving process at their own pace. Without knowing it, those who are farther along may expect the other family members to be where they are in the grieving process. Those who are taking more time may feel there is something wrong with them. Family members less affected by the loss may be less sympathetic and supportive to those who feel the loss more acutely. Lack of support during the holidays can cause the bereaved to feel abandoned by the ones they trust the most.

All of the politics of protection that exist within families come into play during holidays. The bereaved may avoid family reunions because they do not want the joyous occasion brought down by their sadness. Family members may avoid the bereaved because they fear they may exacerbate the bereaved's pain.

Finally, people carry emotional baggage from childhood. All sorts of conflicts and unresolved issues from childhood are carried into adulthood. Family reunions bring the bereaved back together with those who let them down or caused them pain earlier in their lives. All these factors can accumulate and heighten the pain of grieving at family reunions and holiday get-togethers.

SADNESS IN A TIME OF JOY. Holidays are celebrations. Those who celebrate are supposed to be happy and joyous. The reality is that many are not. For many, a holiday is just another day of loneliness, pain, and fear. Approximately two million people die annually in the United States. Even if only a few people were affected by each death, that would still mean that millions of people are grieving each year who weren't grieving the year before.

Grief is not suspended during holidays. Nevertheless, the bereaved feel their sadness is out of place, and they feel left out of the celebration. They may miss the way they used to feel about the holiday. Even if a grieving person begins to have some fun during a holiday, such fun may have a negative result. Good feelings may cause the bereaved to feel guilty, and sad feelings quickly return. When the bereaved are able to once again feel good about feeling good, they should take it as a sign that they are resolving their grief.

HOLIDAY MUSIC. Music brings back memories—memories that remind us of what was and can never be again. Music moves us; it penetrates the walls we have built around ourselves to protect us from the invasion of memories.

During holidays, especially in December, music is everywhere: on the radio, on television specials, in churches, in retail stores, even on telephones while you wait on hold. The bereaved are unable to escape the music that stirs unwelcome memories and emotions.

RELIGIOUS CELEBRATIONS. Most holidays are also Holy Days, and so have a religious and spiritual element. The religious aspect of holidays can be hard for the bereaved to accept. They often are angry with their God during this time of loss and grief. The bereaved may feel abandoned by their God and reluctant to participate in religious ceremonies. The death of a loved one can shake the deepest faith.

Bereaved persons may also feel abandoned by their faith community during holidays; they may feel that their fellow believers are not there for them when they need them most. After all, everyone is busy during the holidays. Also, the clergyperson who leads the holiday services may be the same person who provided pastoral counseling right after the loved one's death, so attending services may remind the bereaved of their loss.

All of the above may cause the hurting survivor to withdraw from the rituals, customs, support, and comfort that their religion once provided. Even worse, they may feel they are suffering another major loss: the loss of faith. Thus, contrary to common wisdom, religious celebrations can sometimes add to holiday woe for the grieving.

FIRST HOLIDAY WITHOUT. Like other "firsts" that the bereaved must recognize and grieve for—the first night without the deceased, the first family get-together, the first meal alone in a restaurant—the first significant holidays must be recognized and grieved for. Important "firsts" loom large in the bereaved's mind. They ask, often weeks ahead of the holiday, "How will I get through the holiday meal or the holiday prayer with the family?"

The day itself is, of course, very difficult. The bereaved find themselves in familiar holiday situations doing familiar things, but without their loved one. Their loss becomes even more real.

"Firsts" are not only hard to look forward to and live through, they are hard to look back on. Once completed, they represent the passage of another landmark on the calendar, and so underline the growing separation from the deceased.

ALCOHOL. Holidays call for celebration, and celebration often calls for alcohol. Because alcohol is a depressant, it is easy to understand why the bereaved should limit their drinking. Alcohol may give quick relief from anxiety, so when the bereaved feel they will be overcome by grief at the family gathering, they might overuse the quick-fix medicine of alcohol. Too much alcohol increases depression, which can cause more drinking. The circle is vicious and can spin out of control.

Sometimes the bereaved discover that physical pain has a way of distracting one from emotional pain. Too much alcohol leads to headache, nausea, and other physical ailments. It is not unheard of for the grieving to drink to cause physical pain in order to distract themselves from emotional pain.

EXHAUSTION. There is much to do during holidays: cleaning the house, cooking the meals, preparing the table, decorating the house, baking the cookies, buying the food, sending the invitations, buying the gifts, planning ceremonies. The list goes on and on, and accomplishing all that needs to be done can be exhausting. There is truth in the old joke about the person who couldn't wait to get back to their job so they could rest up from the holidays.

The job of grieving, by itself, is an exhausting task. The grieving person must not only strive to come to terms with the loss of their loved one, but also with all the little losses in their life that come with that greater loss. The mental work involved seems endless and is very hard.

When the work of the holidays is combined with the task of grieving, the bereaved can feel overwhelmed. They may not have the energy to do either job, let alone both, during holidays.

EXPECTATIONS OF THE "OLD ME." Grief work is also the work of identifying the new self, the self that will live on after suffering the loss of a loved one. Holidays, on the other hand, are often a time when we are asked to be our old self.

Celebrations, customs, rituals, and people that once met the needs of the old self no longer seem to meet the needs of the emerging new self. The bereaved often feel confused during this time and vacillate between the "old me" and the "new me." Thoughts like "I should be putting up the tree, but this year I'd rather decorate the window" or "I should have all the old friends over for the traditional get-together, but I'm just inviting my three best friends this year to share a meal" are examples of this conflict. The "shoulds" are the "old me" speaking, and the new decisions are the "new me" asserting itself. The bereaved often feel guilty because they cannot meet both the old needs and the new needs, and the guilt adds to their holiday stress.

Remember, mourning knows no season; it will occur with or without the holidays. Understanding the above ten reasons why the bereaved sometimes feel worse during holidays may help them to feel less confused, lonely, and sad during their holiday season. The following suggestions may also provide help.

PLAN TO BE SAD. Set aside some time during the day when you are best able to meditate. Light a candle, and think and feel all you can about your grief. I suggest you do it early in the day and take care of the sadness so you are in charge of it; otherwise, you may worry all day that the grief will sneak up on you and knock you down.

BE WITH THOSE YOU WANT TO BE WITH. You know which people are good for you, and you know which take a lot of energy to be around. Choose, if you can, to be around those that are good for you, those who best understand your grief. You are feeling miserable enough without inviting miserable people to be around you, too.

BUY A PRESENT FOR YOURSELF. Give to yourself first. You have been without for too long, and you really deserve something. If nothing else, give yourself the gift of time. Set aside an hour every day for reading, walking, watching television, lunching with a friend, or doing whatever it is you desire to do.

PLAN TO EXPRESS YOUR FEELINGS. If your feelings come to the surface, plan to express them. You don't need to suck it up to protect others. Neither do you need to let your feelings take over your life. Just feel and express as the need arises, and then go on.

PLAN TO ENJOY, AND PLAN TO FEEL GUILTY. When we grieve, we often try to limit our joy in order to limit our guilt. Be prepared for the guilt, but don't let it stop you from enjoying what you can. Remember, when you enjoy yourself, you are beginning to feel good again about feeling good. Take it as a sign that you are working through the grief process.

IF YOU NEED PROFESSIONAL HELP, GO GET IT TODAY. Sometimes a few bits of advice from a professional can save you weeks of worry and grief.

DO IT DIFFERENTLY. Do something you never used to do during this holiday. Take in a play, visit a homeless shelter, take a trip, volunteer for something you never would have volunteered for five years ago.

DON'T OVERDO. Reduce your work load. If you send cards, send them only to those you never see during the year. Decorate one room instead of the whole house. Give gift certificates instead of shopping for presents. Invite guests for lunch instead of dinner. Get your rest.

TALK ABOUT THE DECEASED. You need to reminisce about holidays with your loved one, so do it. If others are uncomfortable talking about the deceased or are uncomfortable about you talking about the deceased, it's their problem.

R.W. Scholes   11/15/96

R.W.SCHOLES   2 / 9 / 99

KEEPING THEIR SPIRIT ALIVE IN OUR FAMILIES: AN AFFIRMATION

Elizabeth Levang and Sherokee Ilse

"My grandmother had a tremendous positive influence in my life. Even after she died, her spirit remained with me. During the birth of my daughter, I knew that Grandma was close by my side; we named Chelsea Maria after her. I'm convinced that her gifts will always be carried on through my daughter. And Chelsea will always know her great grandmother, as we keep her memory alive."

Cindy Leines,
in loving memory of her grandmother, Maria Erickson.

Many of us may wish to carry our loved one with us in spirit. We may choose to do this at family times and special events like reunions, weddings, births, funerals, and holidays. We may seek ways to bring their memory and presence into our family's lives by passing on their names, like Cindy did, by carrying on certain traditions, or by sharing their special sayings and keepsakes with others.

I will remind myself of the ways I keep my loved one's spirit alive in our family, especially during special times. I can honor their memory by passing on their traditions, sayings, and keepsakes.

Reprinted with permission of Fairview Press from *Remembering with Love* by Elizabeth Levang, Ph.D., and Sherokee Ilse. ©1992 by Elizabeth Levang and Sherokee Ilse.

KAREN DORSHIMER-CHAPLIN is an ordained pastor in the United Church of Christ and a chaplain certified by the Association of Professional Chaplains. She earned her Bachelor of Arts degree in psychology from Southeastern Massachusetts University and received her Master of Divinity degree from Andover Newton Theological School. She also completed a two-year residency in Clinical Pastoral Education at Hennepin County Medical Center, in Minneapolis. She is currently employed as a chaplain with Fairview Southdale Hospital in Minneapolis.

Karen lives in the Twin Cities with her husband and their German Shorthaired Pointer. She was raised in Massachusetts and learned to love the beauty of Cape Cod from her father, who died in 1988 from Lou Gehrig's disease. Karen has found solace in her own grief by taking long walks along the beaches of the Cape.

A FAMILY PLAN
FOR THE HOLIDAYS   *Karen Dorshimer-Chaplin*

SCHEDULE A FAMILY MEETING to plan for the upcoming holidays. Developing a plan will help you to feel more in control of your life during this difficult time and will help you to deal with the apprehension of the first holidays without your loved one.

INVOLVE CHILDREN AND TEENS in your planning process. Invite differences of opinion as it is helpful to identify different expectations to avoid conflict during the holidays.

ENCOURAGE EVERYONE to identify three activities that are most important to them for the holidays. Then you will be able to prioritize your activities as a family.

IDENTIFY THE HOLIDAY ROLES of the loved one who has died. Are others willing to accept some of these roles now, or do you need to make changes in some of your traditions for this year? Would you like to develop a family ritual to remember your loved one during this holiday season?

REMEMBER TO BE FLEXIBLE when you plan for the holiday season. The plans made for this year may be changed next year to better meet your needs.

AFTER THE HOLIDAYS, evaluate how the plan worked for your family. Are there some new traditions you would like to keep for next year? Are there traditions that you changed and missed this year?

CARING FOR CHILDREN   *Karen Dorshimer-Chaplin*

CHILDREN NEED A CERTAIN AMOUNT OF ROUTINE in their lives, and often our routines are changed after a loved one's death. Prepare children ahead of time for changes in their routines during holidays.

CHILDREN OFTEN HAVE "MAGICAL THINKING" and may believe that they were the cause of a loved one's death. Children may need additional reassurance during the holidays that they are not to blame for a loved one's death or changes in their family's life following the death of a loved one.

CHILDREN TEND TO EXPRESS THEIR FEELINGS AND EMOTIONS THROUGH THEIR BEHAVIOR. Remember that children may go back to familiar behaviors of a younger age during times of increased stress in their lives.

CHILDREN GRIEVE, TOO! Offer children opportunities to express their feelings and fears. Invite their involvement in creating family rituals and in planning for the holidays.

CHILDREN MAY NEED SOME ADDITIONAL ONE-ON-ONE TIME during the holidays from adults who care about them. This may be an opportunity to accept help from family or friends as you also need to care for yourself during this time.

CARING FOR YOURSELF
Karen Dorshimer-Chaplin

CARE FOR YOURSELF with the same love, acceptance, and nurturing that you offered your loved one in his or her time of need. Healing through grief is a process that takes place gradually and through many seasons.

DISCOVER WHAT BRINGS YOU PEACE, CALM, AND INNER STRENGTH at this time. Trust your inner voice and listen to the needs of your body.

REMEMBER THAT THERE IS NO RIGHT OR WRONG WAY TO GRIEVE. Honor your need for solitude, and honor your own timetable for grieving.

REDUCE STRESS during the holiday season. Allow yourself to say "no" to commitments and events that seem stressful to you.

TREAT YOURSELF TO SOMETHING SPECIAL when you are ready to do so. This is in no way disrespectful to your loved one. It is simply caring for yourself.

AFFIRM YOURSELF as you learn new skills and new responsibilities. Give yourself credit each time you accomplish something new for the first time.

SURROUND YOURSELF WITH PEOPLE who accept you wherever you are in your own journey.

A PERSONAL HOLIDAY PLAN *Karen Dorshimer-Chaplin*

It may be helpful to develop a personal plan for the holidays that will empower you to cope in creative ways with this difficult season or with other special days. Some questions for reflection are suggested below.

WHAT DO I ANTICIPATE will be the "rough waters" of my holidays? Who are some of the people that will be able to carry me over these rough waters?

WHAT ARE SOME OF THE SPECIFIC STRATEGIES that have helped me navigate rough waters during other times in my life? How might I use these strategies during the holidays?

WHICH HOLIDAY TRADITIONS are most important to me this year? Are there some "holiday jobs" that I might delegate to others?

WHICH HOLIDAY TRADITIONS might I skip this year to reduce the stress of the holidays?

WHAT HELP OR SUPPORT might I offer a friend who is grieving during the holidays? What help or support might I seek out from others?

WHAT IS THE SPIRITUAL SIGNIFICANCE of the holidays for me? What people, places, or practices nurture my spirit during the holidays?

WHAT DEMANDS ON MY ENERGY and time would I like to say no to this holiday season?

WHAT IS SOMETHING that I have always wanted to do during the holidays?

WHAT ARE SOME OF MY FAVORITE holiday memories? What are some of the traditions I would like to continue?

WHAT IS SOMETHING SPECIAL I could plan for *after* the holidays?

HOLIDAY RITUALS

Karen Dorshimer-Chaplin

Many families have found healing during the holidays by creating personal ceremonies or rituals that help them to remember their loved one. Children often find comfort through creating personal ceremonies that give them concrete ways to remember their loved one. Some suggestions for the holiday season include:

CREATE A MEMORY BOOK about your loved one. You can include photos, pictures drawn by children, special memorabilia, and stories.

START A NEW TRADITION—for example, a storytelling time to reminisce about your loved one. Children may enjoy hearing stories about the childhood years of a parent or grandparent.

DECORATE AN ORNAMENT OR CANDLE in memory of your loved one.

INVITE FAMILY AND FRIENDS to send you letters and stories about your loved one.

LIGHT CANDLES in honor of your loved one at the holiday table or at a special place in your home.

WRITE LETTERS to your loved one and place these in a special basket or perhaps in a holiday stocking. Children may want to write about events that were important to them during the past year. The letters may be burned to protect privacy.

PREPARE A FAVORITE RECIPE OR MEAL in memory of your loved one.

MAKE OR BUY A GIFT in memory of your loved one to donate to a charity that is important to your family.

BECKY PANSCH, MT-BC, has been the music therapist for Fairview Hospice since February 1996. Before entering health care, she worked in educational settings and private practice. Becky has a music education degree from St. Olaf College, and completed her music therapy training at the University of Minnesota. She is certified by the National Certification Board for Music Therapists.

I've always said I would rather sing an entire concert than speak in public for five minutes. Perhaps that is because my mother put me on a stage to sing almost before I could speak. It has been four years since my mother's death. I think about her often when I sing for patients. It is my way of honoring the gift of music she gave to me. On her birthday my children and I still sing Happy Birthday to her. When we visit her grave, we sing the only hymn she ever wrote. These little musical rituals always bless us by bringing smiles and memories.

THE SEASON OF HOPE

Becky Pansch

It's the sea - son of hope— It's the sea - son of mem - o - ries It's the sea - son to hold— on to the past— while mov - ing on,— Sea - sons come and go— Time chang - es all— we know— New lives e - volve— we find re - solve— and heal - ing starts to grow. Lis - ten to your heart now, Lis - ten while we sing, Lis - ten to the thoughts— and prayers your friends this sea - son bring.—

R.W. SCHOLES   2/25/98

MOTHER'S DAY
AND FATHER'S DAY

Rachel Faldet is an English instructor at Luther College in Decorah, Iowa. After her second miscarriage, she wrote informally and formally in response to grief. She is co-editor of *Our Stories of Miscarriage: Healing With Words*, a collection of essays, journal excerpts, and poems written in response to pregnancy loss.

MOTHER'S DAY: A BITTERSWEET DAY FOR SOME WOMEN

Rachel Faldet

WHEN I THINK OF MOTHER'S DAY, a wealth of images comes to mind.

I see women in restaurants wearing corsages of red roses and babies' breath pinned close to their hearts: visual symbols of motherhood.

I see my mother in the 1960s, wearing a flower-covered puffy hat and a cream-colored coat fastened with buttons the size of half-dollars, three children trailing behind her on Mother's Day morning. As usual, we are late for church.

But I also see women who are not wearing corsages, who may not be walking with children. These women carry in their hearts a quiet, lonesome sadness. They are everywhere: in office buildings, in grocery stores, in libraries, in movie theaters, in airplanes traveling to new destinations.

They are women who have had miscarriages. I am one of them: part of a sisterhood of unspoken sorrow.

One out of five confirmed pregnancies ends in miscarriage. Approximately half a million women miscarry annually. Although miscarriage is common, it is often a taboo topic of conversation. Women who have miscarried are not sure if they should mention their loss to anyone. Pregnancy, childbirth, and menopause get more public attention.

Women are often not prepared for the complex feelings of loss and grief they must cope with when a baby dies within the first twenty weeks of pregnancy. According to Fran Rybarik, director of

Bereavement Services/RTS in La Crosse, Wisconsin, when pregnancy ends in miscarriage, "The whole person is affected—physically, emotionally, socially, and spiritually." A parent invests emotion and hope in a child's life long before it is born.

One day a woman is pregnant; the next day she isn't. Unless she has had multiple miscarriages, her doctor is unlikely to order the tests that might find out the reason for unsuccessful pregnancy. Even then, the medical staff may not be able to give her answers.

Sometimes only a few family members and friends know of the pregnancy; sometimes no one knows except the father. Through tangled emotions, it is hard for a woman to say, "I was pregnant a few days ago, but now I'm not. This is terribly sad for me." Society does not often acknowledge miscarriage as a death that can—and should—be mourned.

People easily sympathize with the death of someone visible, someone whose passage has been marked in legal records, someone with a name. People say, "I'm sorry." They expect mothers—and fathers—to grieve. They encourage them to talk. They are compassionate listeners. They offer tangible solace: a gift of food, a lilac bush to plant in the backyard, an appropriate book.

On Mother's Day it is appropriate to acknowledge a woman's loss—particularly if the miscarriage is recent. But even for women who, with the passage of time, have come to terms with their loss, Mother's Day can bring back a sadness. A simple note written on a blank card and sent in the mail is an act of kindness on this day.

For women who have miscarried, thinking about the lost child is inevitable on Mother's Day. They are confronted with rows of greeting cards in gift shops, restaurant advertisements urging early reservations for Mother's Day brunch, phone companies reminding people to call mothers who are far away, and bouquets of long-lasting carnations delivered to neighbors' houses. The day of celebration is obvious.

As women think about their own mother, they again are reminded of the child or children they do not have. It is bittersweet.

Mother's Day can also be a day of healing.

Women who have miscarried a child should give themselves permission to grieve. They can read about miscarriage, putting themselves in the company of others who have experienced this common, but often publicly unspoken, loss. Reading helps women put their personal sorrow in a larger context: they are not alone. They can talk to family and friends: given the chance, people will reveal the circumstances of their own losses with vividness and compassion. A woman can write about her miscarriage. She can keep her writing private or let others read it. Through writing, no matter how informal it is, she can put some sort of control on the uncontrollable. Because it is spring, a woman can plant a rosebush, a maple tree, or a deep red peony in the yard: a visual symbol of "almost" motherhood.

On Mother's Day, I think about women whose lives have been affected by miscarriage. Perhaps their hearts, like mine, have mended over time. Perhaps their pain is fresh and their heartache needs to be acknowledged by friends and family. Let us use this holiday to help the healing.

MOTHER'S DAY

by Patti Fochi,
in memory of her son, Justin

A day to celebrate motherhood
and I do celebrate
My two daughters fill my world with joy
I rejoice in their beings, their growth
Yet . . . there is a sadness
an emptiness
A place in this mother's heart
for the son, not living
An emptiness, never filled
a quiet reserved place
An emptiness

Reprinted with permission of Fairview Press from *Remembering with Love* by Elizabeth Levang, Ph. D., and Sherokee Ilse. ©1992 by Elizabeth Levang and Sherokee Ilse.

FATHER'S DAY

Jim Nelson,
in loving memory of David

Sunday is Father's Day, and I feel awkward about it.

On a cold morning in January, our son, David, was born,

and I became a father.

Before that cold day ended our son was dead.

Was I a father still?

I had dreams for him,

hopes for him,

love for him, longed for him,

missed him achingly

as only a father could.

Did the grieving and the longing and the missing

achingly

make me a father still,

though I no longer had the relationship or the function?

Father's Day is coming...

I am feeling confused and awkward about it.

Today is Sunday. Father's Day.

A friend approaches me and says,

"Today must be terribly hard for you."

Then he gives me a hug, a heartfelt embrace, and says,

"I'll be thinking of you today. Happy Father's Day."

Suddenly, the awkwardness and confusion is gone.

I am a father.

I will always be one.

Reprinted with permission of Fairview Press from *Remembering with Love* by Elizabeth Levang, Ph. D., and Sherokee Ilse. ©1992 by Elizabeth Levang and Sherokee Ilse.

R.W. Scholes   11/19/96

MEMORIAL DAY

MAKING THE MOST OUT OF MEMORIAL DAY

Elizabeth Levang

MEMORIAL DAY IS OUR national day of mourning. Since the Civil War, the nation has set aside Memorial Day, or Decoration Day as it was formerly known, as a holiday for giving tribute to Americans who died in the service of our country. Memorial Day is a day of remembering, a day to offer thanks, a day to honor those courageous men and women whose death has given us life.

To prepare for this holiday, the staff at cemeteries all across the country brush aside winter's last remains, beautifying and reviving the grounds. Many plan patriotic services to give tribute to the dead while reminding families and friends that their loved ones did not die in vain, that they are remembered and recognized. At cemeteries all across the country, families and friends of the deceased visit over the Memorial Day weekend. Many of these people participate in special patriotic services, while many others walk the grounds to place a wreath or flowers on their loved one's grave.

Memorial Day validates our right to mourn the death of those we love. On no other day of the year is this right so expressly given. Originally specified as a day to memorialize service personnel, Memorial Day now honors and remembers all who have gone before us in death. It allows all of us, as a community and as a nation, the opportunity to publicly demonstrate the love—and the pain—we feel for those who have died.

Memorial Day can be a time of significant healing, which is likely one of the reasons the holiday was first established. Observing Memorial Day can lead to a kind of rebirth and a renewed investment in life as we honor our loved ones, remembering all the ways in which they have touched and enriched our lives. Many families who observe Memorial Day at public functions or in private traditions report feeling better having done so. They often have a cathartic experience that leads to new strength and a feeling of hopefulness about life.

Here are a few tips to make the most out of this national day of mourning and some suggestions for giving tribute:

1. Memorial Day has been set aside for you; it is your day. Spend some time beforehand deciding what you would like to do and with whom. Perhaps you will want to participate in formal ceremonies or maybe plan your own personal remembrance. The key is to do what feels most comfortable and appropriate for you.

2. Let yourself remember your loved one—the laughter and the pain—and share these memories with others. Remembering is vital to healing, for by remembering we let our loved one continue to live on in us and in the world.

3. Allow yourself to express your feelings. So often we think of crying or feeling sad as being negative. Yet without despair we will not feel joy, without the thorn there is no rose. Your feelings demonstrate the depth of your love. Summon the courage to set these feelings free.

4. Know that you are not alone. Take comfort and strength from knowing that people all across the country are united with you on this special day.

5. Be kind to yourself. Grief wears you down. Be realistic about the amount of physical and emotional energy that will be required. Don't overdo things and be sure to include relaxation and some enjoyable activities in your Memorial weekend plans.

R.W. SCHOLES   1 / 29 8/98

MARY LOGUE has written two novels: *Red Lake of the Heart* and *Still Explosion*; two books of poetry: *Discriminating Evidence* and *Settling*; and two books of nonfiction: *A House in the Country* and *Halfway Home: A Granddaughter's Biography*. She has also written many children's books and a young adult novel titled *Dancing with an Alien*.

Of the following poem, "Memorial Day," she writes:

Many years ago, I bought a house in a small river town in Wisconsin, where we started a family tradition—that my father would come to visit on Memorial Day. Later, when he was very ill from a brain tumor, we gathered for our last Memorial Day together. He died on Labor Day that same year. In "Memorial Day," I write about making a memorial, of remembering—in this case—with flowers. Every year the lilacs bloom, the crab apple trees produce hundreds of fragrant flowers. No matter how hard the year has been, they bloom again.

Of her poem, "Giving Thanks for the Turkey," which appears on pages 128–129, Mary writes:

Thanksgiving has always been a hard holiday for my family. Both my mother's mother and her brother died right before Thanksgiving. Then, years apart, my brother and sister were killed a day or two before Thanksgiving. It became a holiday to contend with, so I took it on— through my poetry. I wrote this poem to examine what it means to give thanks. I came to see in writing "Giving Thanks for the Turkey" that we cannot separate the good from the bad. They are tied together in ways that are natural and healthy. Our lives must be filled with both.

MEMORIAL DAY

Mary Logue

I

Three days of shrouded sky.
Below it we open up the ground
and stick flowers in
a pattern which is pleasing
to the eye when seen from above.

Bending and rising, we finally worship
what we ought: the land, the rising warmth,
the spirit that runs in us like sap,
the energy that makes life fill out
the fans of a day lily.

II

Two crab apple trees
in such full bloom the eye wearies
of tracing the petals that lace the
fretwork of branches. Silent music
of soft pink petals. I try to
imagine a person suddenly budding
from every pore—such a great beauty!
We would declare hosanna.

Reprinted with permission of Mid-List Press from *Settling* by Mary Logue. ©1997 by Mary Logue.

III

One year ago today
we gathered on the back lawn:
our family, three daughters and a tired
father. His body thinned to awkward grace,
hands floated to carry a cigarette to lips.
We all knew it would not happen again.
The dogs chased each other on the grass
and his eyes flew after them.

IV

No parents left, we plant flowers
and water trees, we lift an eye
to empty sky, a freighted gray,
we give the day away, a waft
of lilac scent, a handful of
petals lent, and remember
what a time we've had.

R.W. SCHOLES   3/27/98

~

THE ANNIVERSARY
OF A LOSS

~

JACQUELINE JULES is a school librarian, book reviewer, and the author of two children's books. Her poetry and prose has appeared in over fifty publications, including *America, Arthritis Today, Class, Cosmopolitan, Woman's World, Santa Barbara Review, Potomac Review, Chaminade Literary Review, Echoes, Skylark,* and *Lullwater Review.*

About her loss, she writes:

On June 20, 1994, Bill Hechtkopf, my husband of seventeen years, went into the bathroom to take a shower. The door closed and shortly afterward I heard a loud thud. I ran into the bathroom and found him lying on the floor looking dazed. He sat up, holding his chest and heaving, unable to speak. His head dropped back onto the floor. I called 911. An emergency crew came, but there was nothing they could do to resuscitate him. He was forty-seven years old. I was ten years his junior. We had two sons, ages nine and thirteen.

Several weeks after the funeral, in a long-distance phone conversation with one of my dearest friends, I discussed my painful adjustment to widowhood. Sympathetically, my friend admitted to me what she thought must be the most difficult part of being a widow. She said she couldn't imagine not having her husband around to talk things over with. My response startled both of us. I confessed that I was still talking to Bill. There was still a lot I wanted to say to him. His body was buried, not our relationship. I continued to communicate with him through poetry. Others may find comfort in letter writing, journal entries, or simply visiting the cemetery. Death removes the person, not the feelings we have. We have a need to communicate with our deceased loved ones, and we should not feel ashamed to do so.

The poem "Anniversary" is one of forty-nine poems I wrote in response to Bill's death. The candle described in the poem is what is known in Jewish tradition as a yahrzeit candle. Jews light them at home every year on the anniversary of a loved one's death. They are designed to burn for twenty-four hours. While I often feel Bill's presence, I felt it most strongly on the third anniversary of his death. Somehow the flickering of the yahrzeit candle conveyed a tranquility I had not felt before. I gazed at the light dancing on the ceiling for a long time that evening. It felt as if Bill was smiling at me. I smiled back. And then I began the poem, "Anniversary."

ANNIVERSARY

Jacqueline Jules

Three years after
the seven-day candle in the tall red glass,
I light a small candle
and consider your existence
in a realm beyond my knowledge.
If life on earth is only one stage in a series,
you could be safe in an ethereal cocoon,
preparing to emerge as a splendid butterfly in Eden.
I'm ashamed to say
your transformation into something better
brought little comfort to me in the beginning,
as I decried my status as a caterpillar,
a frightened worm, vulnerable to a large and hungry bird.

Living without you
was never as difficult
as living with your death.
The burial of a face
that still smiles at me in photographs
seemed, at times, slightly less credible
than spaceships landing on my lawn.
If I believed in death before,
it was the same way I believed in another universe
and other life forms—somewhere out there—
I wasn't prepared . . .

To light a candle every year in place of going out to dinner,
seeing a play or planning a party. This summer
would have marked twenty years together.
Would we have gone dancing? A little circle
of light flickers on the ceiling, waltzing with the shadows.
I smile. You are dancing for me,
whirling in the endless light of memory.

GINNY STANFORD is an artist and writer living in Sebastopol, California. Her paintings hang in the National Portrait Gallery in Washington, D.C., and in public and private collections throughout the U.S. She is represented by Somerhill Gallery, in Chapel Hill, North Carolina, and Portraits, Inc., in, New York. Her nonfiction has appeared in *New Orleans Review, New Letters,* and elsewhere. Ginny is currently at work on a novel.

My husband took his life on June 3, 1978, in Fayetteville, Arkansas. He shot himself in the chest with a .22 revolver. At the time of his death at age 29, Frank Stanford had published five collections of poetry: The Singing Knives, Ladies From Hell, Field Talk, Shade, Arkansas Bench Stone, *and a 542-page poem,* The Battlefield Where the Moon Says I Love You. *His posthumous books include* Crib Death, You, The Light the Dead See, *and a volume of short fiction,* Conditions Uncertain and Likely to Pass Away. *In the early 1970s he collaborated on an award-winning documentary film about his own life and work titled,* It Wasn't a Dream It Was a Flood. *Frank Stanford was the founding editor of Lost Roads Publishers.*

I don't necessarily consider myself a model of how to cope with such a loss. If I had it to do over again, there are many things I'd do differently. Frank's reputation as a legendary figure and gifted poet has continued to grow over the years. That's made the loss easier to bear. His work lives on and continues to affect people deeply.

I'm still coping. I miss Frank. I've coped by living my life day by day — by just getting up in the morning, having tea, and going to work, when that's all I could do. I've translated a lot of my anger, longing, and sadness into art. That's helped tremendously. I feel particularly connected to Frank when I'm writing.

The holidays are often difficult enough without death intervening. My first Christmas as a widow I spent in New York City; my second on a train to California. I decided to make the traditional family holidays like Christmas and Thanksgiving opportunities to have new experiences. I found great freedom and comfort in that, and I've continued my own tradition of celebrating holidays in a unique way.

It has taken me a very long time to understand that love is more powerful than death, and to realize that Frank is still with me. Everyone must make their own way through grief and loss, but, if I could give advice to others, especially survivors of suicide, I'd urge them to seek counseling if they feel overwhelmed by guilt. I'd also urge them to be receptive to the connection that will always exist between them and their loved one. It's no longer of this world, no longer physical, but it's real, powerful, and transforming. My visceral recognition of that truth has, finally, made my life blossom. Death does not have to be the end.

DEATH IN THE COOL EVENING   *Ginny Stanford*

I'VE ALWAYS CALLED IT LOVE AT FIRST SIGHT, the compelling visceral attraction that overpowers competing instincts, any tendency to caution or reason. When Frank said hello, I fell in love with his voice. By the end of that day, I was sure I loved everything he had been, was then, would ever be. He was wildly enthusiastic about my painting—there's nothing like being understood. In the weeks that followed I read from his manuscripts and made drawings based on the poems. He bought me notebooks and different kinds of pens to try out.

"Paint an old man sitting by a coffin waving at the moon; a fat lady shelling peas and a centaur behind her; a blind Gypsy holding a conch shell. Paint a white horse breaking away from a funeral hearse; a scarecrow wearing a kimono. Paint smoke rings," he said.

Back then I was sure of many things. I believed Frank and I would always be together, and that time would only bring us more of what we wanted, as if the course of our lives had been set to trace an unwavering line upward toward happiness and achievement.

I have never regretted leaving the Midwest, although sometimes I miss the farm—our rambling house with the front porch that wrapped around two sides, the elaborate garden we had, all the land. Sometimes I miss the prairie and its views of each day's beginning and end. I loved watching that sky. Things are different in Northern California. Coastal hills, ghosts of old mountain ranges barricade the eastern horizon. I don't see the copper edge of the

Reprinted with permission of Fairview Press from *When a Lifemate Dies,* edited by Susan Heinlein, Grace Brumett, and Jane-Ellen Tibbals. ©1997 by Susan Heinlein, Grace Brumett, and Jane-Ellen Tibbals.

moon rising out of the earth like I used to, but nothing the Midwest has to offer can compare with the sight of that enormous red crescent sinking into the Pacific in the middle of the night.

Bodega Head is where I go to watch the moon set—November and December are the best months. I've never been scared to take the path on the crest of those high cliffs alone late at night. Perhaps I should be. A buck deer and I met once in the dark; I saw the white smoke coming out of his nostrils before I saw him.

Frank had been the one so at home around water. I never thought I'd end up feeling the same way. Now I can't imagine leaving here. Living on the western edge of this continent, so far away from where I began, is reassuring to me now—the whole country behind me; two mountain ranges, two time zones, and eighteen years now lay between me and the hot, oppressive summer of his death. I've had plenty of time to go over that Saturday, wonder why I didn't see it coming, parse every sentence I uttered—every word—comb through everything I did but wish I hadn't, and everything I wanted to say but didn't. As if my taking out one part could have changed the outcome.

He died before I had time to finish his portrait.

In May he said, "Copy this Gauguin and paint me standing in front of it. Call it 'Spirit of the Dead Watching.'" A Tahitian girl is clutching her pillow in fear, her bed a sumptuous pattern of blue, rose, yellow, and bright orange. A spray of phosphorescent flowers decorates the wall behind her. At the foot of the bed is another woman, hooded, dressed in black. She sits, staring impassively ahead. She is manao tupapao, the spirit of the dead watching. I thought it was a great idea. I thought he had the best ideas.

"Why don't you pose in your kimono?" I said.

We buried him barefoot in that kimono. At first, the funeral home refused. They insisted he wear a suit and shoes; claimed it was a state law. Sometime in the weeks after his death I rolled up the canvas and placed it in a corner of my parent's attic where it remains.

"I love you," was the last thing he said to me. He said I love you, and I said, "Don't give me that crap."

Saturday evening. June third. He had betrayed me by having an affair and I had found out. I was hurt and humiliated and angry enough to put him through a wall. I love you. It was the first time I didn't automatically answer back, I love you, too. I barely tolerated the hug he tried to give me, my arms stiff at my sides. He tried to kiss me, and I turned my head so that his lips only grazed my hair. Then he left. Forever. He left me in a room and shut the door behind him as he left. He took three steps across a hall into another room and shut another door and shot himself.

In the span of the longest five or six seconds I have ever lived through, Frank fired three shots into his chest. Three pops, three cries. All I had was sound. I couldn't see him; I could only imagine what he was doing in another part of the house. With the sound of the first shot, time stopped, changed course, and went backward through the second and third shots, then reconstructed itself into an endless, directionless loop. Before Saturday, June third, time was a straight line. After Saturday, a loop.

I heard a sharp crack, a hard slap, an angry teacher breaking his ruler against a desk. I heard the crack and just as sharp I heard Frank hollering, "Oh"—surprised. I heard him step on a copperhead, get stung by a yellow jacket, smash his thumb with a hammer. I watched him jump into Spider Creek, heard him hit the cold water and yelp from the shock. Pop, Oh! Pop, Oh! Pop, Oh!

After the third cry I knew he was dead. Imagine the wall is telling you a bedtime story. Go to sleep now, it might say. That is how the news was delivered. A quiet voice from somewhere inside me said flatly, It's all over; he's killed himself. I didn't want to move.

But the same silent voice was ordering me out. Get out, get out, it kept repeating. Call the police.

I didn't want to look. He's blown his brains out, the voice said. Don't go in there. Save the memory.

Death had changed his eyes from hazel to pale porcelain green. I climbed onto the bed where he lay and sat astride his crooked body, amazed at the sight of three small red holes ringing his heart. I put my hands on his chest. While I waited for the police, I tried to memorize every detail of his face before I never saw it again. He looked through me toward a distant place, and I tried wishing myself there. This is real, I repeated, working hard to convince myself; this is real, this is real.

I spent the night in a Holiday Inn. I was afraid to close my eyes, afraid to dream, afraid to let sleep seal the day and lock it into history. Tomorrow, I thought, he will be irretrievable. Finally, against my will, I slept, and not fitfully as I had expected, but deeply. During that long deep sleep—more like a coma—I didn't dream about Frank. I didn't dream at all. He sent no messages, instructions, or last requests and I felt no trace of our connection.

His funeral was like every funeral—inadequate. Stand up. Sit down. Kneel. Pray. Get used to it. I remember the missal in my lap. It was a deep, lush, luminous red. The soles of my black shoes clacked on marble tiles, each step echoing through cavernous silence as I made my way to a pew. What I remember most clearly is Frank's casket—so small and far away—bathed by a pool of dim light. It glowed in the darkness of the church like Sleeping Beauty's glass coffin. I see thick white candles burning in giant brass candlesticks at his head and feet. I think of a clearing in the forest, and all the animals in a circle waiting for Sleeping Beauty to open her eyes.

I don't know if the first year was the worst, but it was the most singular. Then death was new—every day unique, the first of its kind to be lived without him—and the point was simply to survive. The first year, I couldn't imagine there would be a second one. I anchored myself to painting and stayed busy. It was hard to concentrate on art because I kept expecting someone to burst through the door of the studio and shoot me. I scoured Frank's poems for ideas and ways to stay close to him.

All that year I looked for windows, mirrors, thin fingers of light, something to slip through, some way to find Frank through faith or will, on the other side of pain. I dreamed of secret passageways, walls that were really doors opening into life, and Frank vibrant, splendidly alive on the other side of those walls. My nights were full of second chances.

What I saw before me was a desert of time, a white monotony of absence and regret that I could never cross. I imagined him waiting at the end of that long first year with fresh water and a laurel wreath, waving from the finish line to spur me on. "You made it," he might say, "and I'm your reward."

For years I saw him—a gesture, a wave, a blur. His promises were everywhere. Set me as a seal upon thine heart, as a seal upon thine arm; for love is strong as death. I thought it was him. I worked hard at forgetting but he stayed with me, beside me, behind me. I felt him waiting, like the fog waits to come in on summer evenings. Just roll in over the hills while I sleep, I told him. You can disappear with the sunrise.

Once I thought I saw him, but it was the light hitting my windshield. I thought I saw him, but it was a blue jay in a bay tree. I thought I saw him, but it was a curtain blowing through a window. I saw a man waiting for the bus and thought it was him. I saw a shadow dancing across a wall and thought it was him. I was expecting him. I had the red carpet out. A black cat jumped down out of a tree and I thought it was him. I heard something like his voice, but it belonged to an owl. I thought I saw him, but it was smoke from a brush pile. I thought it was him, but it was my longing, my regret. Sometimes when the phone rang I imagined he might be calling. I said, "I love you, too." I said it often in case he might be listening.

I studied the photographs I'd taken, looking for clues, and found the other woman in his face. At the point where she entered our lives I saw lies cross-hatching, shadowing his cheeks, filling in below his eyes with darkness. The smile began fading in and out; it grew less frequent. Finally his jaw became a clenched fist, clamped down tight on honesty, choking it back; his face seemed fossilized. He looked driven, wild, worn out in the last pictures. I decided she had killed him.

The fifth summer I opened one of his books and read a poem on the last page and I remembered our life purposefully. To console myself I painted a meadow like the meadow at the farm—prairie hay turning copper in October light, intersecting an eastern sky infiltrated by the beginnings of darkness. I painted my longing as a red silk kimono with its pattern of tiny pink and white gourds, floating above the tall grass. The seventh summer I took off my wedding ring and put it in a pine trunk. The eighth summer I gave all his records to the library. I couldn't bear to listen to the music of our life. The tenth summer I wore his Saint Francis medal.

I painted his portrait during the thirteenth summer and we became friends again. I began to celebrate his birthday once more.

On the fourteenth anniversary of his suicide I fired a twenty-two revolver at a paper target. It felt a little like murder. Did you feel the pain? How were you able to keep pulling the trigger? Why didn't you drop the gun? Why did you leave? I hit the bull's eye twice.

Three months later, on August first, I celebrated his birthday for the first time in a long while. Instead of a cake, I bought a package of twelve-inch red tapers. I collected all the candlesticks in the house and arranged them in a circle on the dining room table and put my bouquet in the center. It had all his favorite flowers: bachelor buttons, mixed with yellow coreopsis and white cosmos, tied with a red ribbon. I'd picked them from the flower bed by the front door. The fog was beginning to roll in and soften the long shadows that fell across my deck. I lit the candles at dusk—fifteen in all—and stepped back to take in the sight. He would get a kick out of this, I thought.

June third comes and goes. I grow older and Frank remains forever twenty-nine. Time has taught me, among other things, that death is persistent and enduring beyond my capacity to imagine it. People still ask me, Why? I used to have an answer. Now I say, I don't know.

The day we met, Frank read me one of his own poems. It remains my favorite simply because it was part of such a remarkable encounter. The irony has not been lost on me.

Death in the Cool Evening

I move
Like the deer in the forest
I see you before you see me
We are like the moist rose
Which opens alone
When I'm dreaming
I linger by the pool of many seasons
Suddenly it is night
Time passes like the shadows
That were not
There when you lifted your head
Dreams leave their hind tracks
Something red and warm to go by
So it is the hunters of this world
Close in.

ANNIVERSARY ANXIETY:
AN AFFIRMATION   *Elizabeth Levang and Sherokee Ilse*

"I can't begin to describe the amount of apprehension and dread my husband and I experienced in anticipation of the first anniversary of our grandchild's death. We had no idea how to make this day easier on us."

Anonymous

As the anniversary date of our loved one's death approaches, many of us become filled with anxiety and tension. We fear having to face that dreadful day and all the reminders associated with it. We want to banish it from the calendar forever, but we know we cannot. Finding a way to get through this difficult day may be uppermost in our mind.

It is normal to feel anxious and apprehensive about our loved one's anniversary date. There are far too many painful memories tied to it. As with many other things in life, though, our worrying and fretting may prove to be more distressing than the actual day. Planning how to spend the time and focusing on the good in our life may be of some help in trying to cope with this troubling time.

It is okay if I feel some apprehension or fear at the impending anniversary of my loved one's death. I can think of how I want to spend the time and make the day easier on me.

Reprinted with permission of Fairview Press from *Remembering with Love* by Elizabeth Levang, Ph.D., and Sherokee Ilse. ©1992 by Elizabeth Levang and Sherokee Ilse.

JANIS KEYSER HEIL, PH.D. is the executive director of
UNITE, Inc., a non-profit organization offering grief
support after the death of a baby. She is also the
director of the Regional Pediatric Bereavement
Resource Center at St. Christopher's Hospital for
Children, where she also serves as hospital bereavement coordinator and chaplain. She is certified as
both a death educator and grief counselor by the
Association for Death Education and Counseling.
Janis began this work in 1980 after the death of her
daughter, Jessica Brooke, who was stillborn at full
term. The UNITE support group was Janis's lifeline
through her grieving and subsequent pregnancy, letting her know she was normal in what she was feeling
and was not alone.

THOUGHTS ON
AN ANNIVERSARY

Janis Keyser Heil,
in memory of Jessica

It's true that she's always in
the back of my mind.
But she's not always on my mind.
When I think of her now, I
remember her warmly.
I rarely cry anymore out of
hurt or anger.
But there are times when something
can throw me right back to that
very day.
And the depth of my feelings of
loss and pain once again equal
the depth of my love for her.
And I cry. And I hurt.
But it reminds me all the more
that she will always be
part of my life, and that she's
special enough to care about.
Time has healed me.
But time has not made me forget.

ALTHA EDGREN is the mother of two healthy, happy, and creative children and has a medical writing business based in St. Paul, Minnesota.

She writes about her loss:

At what we assumed would be a routine ultrasound examination to determine the gestational age of our "surprise pregnancy" baby, a doctor we had never met before told us our fourteen-week-old fetus was severely deformed and had no chance of survival. She was anencephalic, developing without a portion of the brain and skull. Even if the pregnancy could be carried to full term, the baby would be stillborn or die within several days of birth. "Coda" was, in fact, a journal entry written one year after we made the very difficult decision to terminate our pregnancy.

In the year after, it seemed, everywhere I turned I was surrounded by women who also had stories of pregnancy loss: the young coworker who lost her baby to miscarriage earlier in the year, the neighbor who finally turned to adoption after several heartbreaking attempts to carry a pregnancy, and the older women who with teary eyes told me that losing a baby just wasn't something you could talk about forty years ago.

In mid-October, I light a candle in remembrance of that tiny spirit that was not able to manifest itself in physical form in this life. There is healing in creating a remembrance ritual, and there is healing in giving words to grief. Don't be afraid to share your story; you may be amazed at the comfort it can bring.

CODA: A JOURNAL ENTRY
ONE YEAR LATER

Altha Edgren

I AM THINKING ABOUT THE BABY at this the one-year anniversary of her passing. About the ultrasound, about seeing her beautiful face, about the doctor telling us she had no chance of survival.

About her leaving me, about all of the women who comforted me with stories of their lost babies, a sorority of sorrow, these women, and now myself among them, moving past the pain to find a jagged peace in comforting another suffering sister.

Reprinted with permission of Fairview Press from *Our Stories of Miscarriage,* edited by Rachel Faldet and Karen Fitton. ©1997 by Rachel Faldet and Karen Fitton.

R. W. Scholes   12/24/97

BIRTHDAYS

R W. SCHOLES   3/19/98

SHEROKEE ILSE has been a publisher and bereavement author since 1982. Among her published books are *Remembering and Empty Arms: Coping with Miscarriage, Stillbirth and Infant Death* and *Remembering with Love: Messages of Hope for the First Year of Grieving and Beyond*. She has personal experience with loss. She is the mother of three babies who died in miscarriage and stillbirth and has had her own mother and very close grandparents die. As a well-respected international lecturer on bereavement, she continues to share her messages of hope, love, and the importance of memories for healing.

She writes:

Living through the loss of a loved one is one of life's greatest challenges. I remember wondering if I would make it, and if I should even try to make it through the pain. The energy that grieving took and the deep sadness in my soul overcame all else in my life for a long time. I wanted to sleep for a year and wake up healed, but no such luck. We can't go around grief, we must go through it. I have since learned that the tough job of missing, loving, remembering, and the anguish, sorrow and anger we feel, is what helps us heal. These emotions honor our loved one and show us and others how much they were, and still are, loved.

Holiday times are especially difficult for those of us who have lost someone, because of the family memories and the hopes we held for future family togetherness. How can life go on so easily with the rest of the world, when our loved one is missing and we have a deep hole in our heart? We are now forever changed and those special days remind us of just how much.

The holidays have rarely been smooth or easy, but they always went better if I gave some thought beforehand about what I wanted to happen on that day. Sometimes I needed to escape. Other times I needed to change the traditions and routines. For instance, at Christmas time I would put special ornaments on the tree, light a candle to remember those who were missing, and seek out a different house to spend the day at. On my stillborn son Brennan's first birthday, I wrote him a poem, visited the hospital where he was born, remembered the details of the day, then went to the place where we scattered his ashes and cried with my husband. The fear and worry before the day were actually worse than the day itself. I believe the day was better because I took charge and did what was in my heart. I told people who I knew would support me what I needed, and they encouraged me to do what felt right.

You are a new and different person, like it or not. Make your feelings and needs known, to yourself and others. Then go with the flow—if you want something done differently, then do it differently. Seek support from those you trust will give it to you; if you need to be left alone or are actually feeling okay about the day, let that happen too. Don't swim up against the rapids; rather, let the river take you where you need to go and do what seems right in your heart. Prepare—take control over that which you can control, and let go of all else that is out of your control. Living through holidays, especially the "firsts" of year one, won't be easy, but you can survive, and it can even be a positive experience. Trust that, as you move forward in spite of your pain and sadness.

HAPPY BIRTHDAY

Sherokee Ilse,
in loving memory of her
grandmother, Genevieve Kriesch

It is your birthday today.
Happy Birthday!
Can't help but think of you,
Wishing we could talk, laugh, play
And remember together.
We would sing "Happy Birthday" to you,
Watch you blow out candles and make a wish.
We might talk of your birth, the past
And dreams of tomorrow.
Instead I shed tears as I smile,
Thinking of the gifts your life
Has given me, our family
And so many others.
Happy Birthday! We miss you.

Reprinted with permission of Fairview Press from *Remembering with Love* by Elizabeth Levang,
Ph. D., and Sherokee Ilse. ©1992 by Elizabeth Levang and Sherokee Ilse.

R.W. Scholes   5/6/97

MOVING DAY

GRACE BRUMETT is a teacher, writer, and musician, and is the mother of three children, ages eighteen to twenty-seven. She earned a degree in psychology from the University of California. She is a student of Zen Buddhism and was once the private literary secretary to Pulitzer Prize-winning poet Gary Snyder.

In 1983 her husband, Michael, was diagnosed with Hodgkins Lymphoma. With treatment the cancer went into remission, but in 1989 it reoccurred. After spending five years in further treatment, her husband died at home on June 17, 1994.

She writes:

*I kept a journal throughout Michael's illness and after his death. My journal has been my outlet and refuge. After Michael's death, I felt compelled to write "Bless This House" in all its raw-ness and heartfelt honesty. As I shared pieces of it with friends, it became obvious that the story might help others. I joined a hos-pice support group for new widows and widowers shortly after Michael died. We told our stories to one another, and in this sim-ple exchange we derived great comfort, which was very healing. Out of this exchange came an anthology of stories—*When a Lifemate Dies: Stories of Love, Loss, and Healing—*which I co-edited and in which "Bless This House" was included.*

Just as my love for Michael will never go away, grief will always be a part of who I am. The first year I was in intense grief. The second year was, in some ways, even harder, as my grief remained intense, but I was receiving less tolerance and understanding from a world that wanted me better right now. But, as time has gone by, the waves of intense grief have become fewer and farther between. I am no longer in that tunnel of pain and sorrow where grief dominates one's total being. My life is full now, filled with new friends and lovers. It's not what I would have imagined or desired. It's simply different.

BLESS THIS HOUSE

Grace Brumett

June 24, 1995

ANOTHER GOOD-BYE stands before me. In a little over a week I will
leave this house for a new one, the first to know my steps without
Michael. I have not yet packed a single box. I don't even have
boxes. All around me lies the disorder of a family's daily chaos—
dirty dishes on the counter, piles of laundry needing to be folded,
dust on the window ledge, stacks of unread books and magazines
on the coffee table, my desk littered with papers I must deal with
someday, unopened junk mail and bills that will need a response—
"Michael Brumett is dead now. Please close the account."

No, I haven't begun to pack yet. I'm in a jumble of emotions I
can't predict or sort. How can I be so passive even as I take big
steps? What keeps me from packing? Is it fear that now I must
begin the hard steps of creating a life that is "mine" and not "ours"?

Am I making wise choices? Would Michael approve? I always
depended on his advice. We made decisions together. Will this
move take me further away from the shreds of us and the life we
had together into the unknown reality of my solitary present life?
Another letting go I must face?

"Grace, you are so strong!" I've heard it said so many times that
it has begun to sound like a curse. Yes, strong. I don't know if fear
is a part of my vocabulary anymore; panic maybe, but fear was
blasted out the door by too many years of watching what one fears
the most happen slowly in front of me—Michael, my mate of
twenty-five years, dying bit by bit.

Reprinted with permission of Fairview Press from *When a Lifemate Dies,* edited by Susan
Heinlein, Grace Brumett, and Jane-Ellen Tibbals. ©1997 by Susan Heinlein, Grace Brumett,
and Jane-Ellen Tibbals.

Now that is done.

DEATH IS NOT THE ENEMY. There is nothing more to fear. Dead is easy. It's the little things, the everyday things that are hard. The living. Like paying the bills on time; paying attention to practical details when I really could care less. Getting my youngest son to school. Fixing the car. How do I get it across town, then to work and back later to retrieve it all by myself?

Losing keys. Where are they? Don't lock myself out. Keeping track of things when I'd rather not be bothered, but panic when I don't. Making all the small decisions and some big ones without my partner to run it by.

And then reminding myself that I must stay soft and compassionate. It would be so easy to slip into hardness, bitterness, cynicism. I hear people agonize over so many mundane silly things, or so it appears to me in my self-indulgent state of mind. "Stop fretting!" I want to scream. Of course, the world will keep turning whether or not little Billy makes the baseball team (and what can you do about it anyway?); whether or not Clinton gets elected or O.J. convicted (and who cares anyway?); whether or not you buy the car (it's only money after all); whether or not adolescent Sara is in a constant, unbearable mood these days (it will pass, I'm sure). It will all work out. It's not the end of the world.

Stay soft, sympathetic, I remind myself. This is important, this stuff of life, even though at this moment in my life it may seem a luxury to worry about small triumphs, tragedies, and conflicts. It would be so easy for me to feel resentful. If they only knew what they have. Everything. Their husband didn't just die.

A world didn't just end.

And then there's that question I have at moments asked myself when I have dared to think of a future: Will I ever find joy in my gut again and the capacity to dream? I am so numb now. Numb and yet, whack!—so wide awake.

Such are the rambles of fresh widow grief that keep me from the business of packing. I must move to a new house. I am propelled by necessity. I can no longer afford this big one. But I also recognize my sense of relief that I didn't have to make this healthy decision to move on. It was made for me, which makes it easier. I may not have had the courage to break my inertia. I like to think the Great Mystery has once again come to my rescue. I've come to trust it that way.

Leaving this house has great significance. It will be my first move alone.

I could just go through the motions and act "normal," but recently I have found the value in honoring my inner journey in my outer life. When something is significant, as all "firsts" tend to be for a new widow, a simple ritual in acknowledgment of steps taken is empowering. So in the midst of all the boxes I must surely pack in this next, last week, I will pause here to do my spiritual packing, to beat a drum, to mark the moment with a little serious silence and a few words of blessing to this house:

They say a house has its own soul, that houses come to us for a purpose. They take care of us, hold us, guard our secrets, contain our passions. When we leave them, we leave a part of ourselves within them.

Indeed, House, what stories you could tell. The first time I stepped inside your door I knew you were a substantial house with a heart big enough to embrace all that was ahead. I sat awhile, asked permission to be here, and you received us. Thank you, House.

Thank you for witnessing these last three magnificent years of passage for my family. I brought Michael to you, it would seem now, in order to die.

And dying takes time. It isn't easy. It's a big deal. I brought him directly from the bone marrow transplant ward at Stanford—that science-fiction battle zone where he spent six weeks in isolation. Even the air wasn't safe for his body. They gave him a lethal dose of chemotherapy so every cell began to die. Then they tried to trick his body and transplanted fresh clean marrow in the hopes that it would multiply and replenish his dying body. We prayed each day, each moment. Me beside him, meticulously masked, gowned and scrubbed down because nothing organic or alive could come near him. We prayed and watched the computer stats hooked to his body along with the morphine drips and sterile food fed into his jugular. We rejoiced at each tiny rise in platelet and white blood cell count they recorded, hardly daring to hope, while not doubting for a moment that all things are possible. Many weeks later he re-entered life for the final stage with his family here in this house. Hopeful. He felt welcome—at home.

Now, the very creak of your stairs, House, is impregnated with images of Michael stubbornly pulling himself up with his own unfailing strength, up to our bed and the intimacy of our room. His salty smell still lingers in my closet. I smile in spite of myself at all the drama you have silently born these last three years. All the midnight-whispered assurances we gave one another as I would watch Michael endlessly, touching his whiskered drawn face over and over in the night, needing to voice again and again one more time, "I love you, Michael."

"I know," he would smile.

All the celebrations with the stream of friends coming to say good-bye. But not really. They came to hold Michael here a little longer with their love.

So many visitors received through your door for merry meals and intimate talks. Reveling in the holiness we all experienced living so close to the fragile veil that separates worlds. Exhilaration and utter exhaustion. And yes, again, the tears and the tears and the tears. All the anxious exchanges you heard with doctors and the announcements received on the phone, "I'm sorry. It's back and there's nothing more we can do." Our rallying cry, as we've always done in affirmation of life: "Then we'll go to Mexico and play!" Excitement within your walls of packing up one more time.

Music, friends, family agonizing each in our own way in explosions of anger, fear, panic, outrage, frustration, and sad and sad and sad. Our tears stained your proud wooden floors.

Good-byes. You witnessed extravagantly wild and crazy gatherings of good-byes with candles lit, incense burning, conversation through the night, people dancing, singing through your rooms, dope and liquor as medicine to loosen our minds and numb our pain. Guitars strumming, fire burning for yet one more, one more celebration of our agony.

You heard rage, harsh words, morphine confusion. You witnessed Michael's Tibetan vajra mysteriously, spontaneously ignite and flame on your hearth as an omen of release. You were patient as we continually redrew the line of hope and laughed yet again in death's face.

You rocked us in the desperate passion of our tender lovemaking, heightened by the inevitable separation looming imminently before us. You were quiet while we held hands in a circle for the very last time physically intact as a family, two days before death's visitation. Extra long. You gave us time.

Oh, House, right here where I sit, Michael drew his very last rasping breath and, with that final look of merging love, took me with him to eternity.

This last long year you have secreted what we have lovingly referred to as Michael's room—the closet shrine with Michael's ashes where each one of us has crept at odd hours to commune with spirit and lick our wounds.

I've walked your rooms now a full turn of the seasons, retracing every step, every memory. Your walls have been safe enough to hold even the darkness of my grief . Now I feel I can let go of these protective walls that have cradled my agony, my sleepless aching nights and vacant lonely days. You have served me well. The images are forever embedded deep within my psyche. The time is right to move on. I know this with a blind faith I have come to accept like a sleepwalker in the dark who somehow doesn't fall. I can close your door gently, firmly now, with the resolve that it is only by shutting one door that another will open.

June 30, 1995

THE HOUSE IS EMPTY NOW. Not one physical vestige of our life here remains. I have picked every tack, marble, and paper clip from the carpets. I have emptied each closet and drawer. I have scoured every inch, wiped every wall and light fixture. I have painted over the wall in my son's room where it exploded through those last weeks as an organic and growing mural of words and images drawn to mirror the pain, anguish, and transformation of a father's dying.

Now I sit, quiet inside and out, hearing only the silent echoes of this passing moment in these empty rooms. I am very still. It is afternoon, 3:45, forever marked for me as the moment of Michael's passing almost to the day a year ago. The light falls on the carpet of my barren room just the way it did at his passing. The same birds are singing sweetly outside, the warm scents of summer plants and the quality of the air evoke an instant connection out of ordinary time and space. I am right there again. Right here.

I bring to this spot a dark red rose I pick from our garden and sit on the empty floor—this spot where Michael left his body. The sunlight on my back through the bedroom window ignites my body. As I feel the touch of hot sun on my spine, there is a great sense of peace that reaches far beyond sadness.

I hear once more Michael's words of blessing he left for his children, spoken one timeless day in his dying:

All is energy.
It doesn't die.
It moves on
But remains one.
It is something
Can't be spoken.
Keep a spiritual side to you.
Look for the good.
I love you and approve.

And it is enough.

ROSH HASHANAH,
YOM KIPPUR,
AND PASSOVER

HOWARD WARSETT is a Certified Public Accountant practicing in Minneapolis. Estee Warsett is an electrologist practicing in New Hope, Minnesota.

Estee describes the loss that inspired their poem:

Our first pregnancy was picture perfect and gave us a beautiful baby boy. A couple of years later we were ready to add to our family. A miscarriage left us feeling empty, but early the next year we were once again pregnant. Like many pregnant couples, we gave a sigh of relief after the first trimester. Little did we know that soon our lives would change forever. I was in my thirty-ninth week of pregnancy. The baby was very active, much more than my first. It was the day before Rosh Hashanah, the Jewish New Year. We were to have family for dinner the next evening, and I was busy all day running errands with a friend to prepare for the holiday. That evening Howard asked how much movement I'd had that day. I stopped in my tracks and commented that I'd had several Braxton Hicks contractions, but I didn't remember a lot of movement. I pushed on my belly and got no response. We thought it was just in our heads. Go to sleep and everything will be okay in the morning. Needless to say, I didn't sleep much that night. At about six in the morning, I called my obstetrician.

I followed his advice to drink orange juice or eat something with sugar to stimulate movement. If there was no response, we were to go to the hospital for tests. Shortly thereafter, with cameras and suitcases in hand, we marched into the hospital. It did not register in our minds that something might be wrong. We were led to a room, and the nurse checked for a heartbeat. When the nurse was unable to hear a heartbeat, our tension and anxiety suddenly increased. With a lump in her throat and holding back a tear, the nurse said she was going to call my doctor.

After greeting Howard and me, my doctor wheeled an ultrasound machine into the room. We quickly saw that there was no heartbeat. My doctor left the room, but the nurse came back to be with us. She said my doctor was also very upset and needed a few minutes alone. When he returned, he said he couldn't believe this had happened to such wonderful parents. He said he would have the lab stand by and do all that he could to find out why this had happened. Labor was induced, and about six hours later I gave birth to a beautiful baby boy.

At the moment of birth, everything was amazingly calm. The lights were turned down. There was a hush in the room. As soon as the baby was delivered, my doctor said that we had our answer. There was a knot in the umbilical cord. In the first trimester of pregnancy, his movements had caused a knot to form. Because he was so active, the knot had tightened, cutting off his oxygen supply. We were grateful to learn this, because only about half of parents who lose a baby ever find out why their child died.

We decided to give our baby a special name, since the name we had originally chosen was for a living child. We named him Baruch, which in Hebrew means "blessed." We truly did feel blessed to have had him even for such a short time. The staff encouraged us to hold him, and for us it was very natural. We took photographs, and on video we each said a special message to him. Our parents came to see him, which meant a great deal to us. They had not only the pain of the loss of a grandchild but also the pain of seeing their own children suffer. We spent several hours with Baruch until we felt it was time to let go.

We chose to have a funeral for Baruch. Another family who had lost a child thoughtfully suggested we bury him with a deceased family member instead of alone in the children's section of the cemetery, so we buried him with my grandmother. Knowing that she was going to be taking care of him brought some comfort. At the funeral, the rabbi remarked that Baruch's "soul was so pure he need not be judged." The days between Rosh Hashanah and

Yom Kippur are the days of judgment during which it is determined whether or not you will be written in the book of life for the following year.

As the years have passed, the gut-wrenching pain that followed Baruch's death has gone away, but a part of me and of my family will always be missing. Hardly a day goes by that I don't think of him. Milestones such as when he would have had a birthday, taken his first steps, or gone to school have been especially difficult.

Our family visits him on his birthday. We bring a rose with baby's breath and spend some time together. His gravestone marker has his name in both Hebrew and English, and says, "Stillborn, September 30, 1989." Further down, the marker reads, "Our forever baby." It took several years, but I finally enlarged and framed some of the beautiful pictures we took the night he was born. Three 5 x 7 pictures are displayed with some of the rest of our family pictures in our family room. On his birthday we watch the video we took in the hospital. I still have a plant that was given to us by a friend on the day of his funeral. The plant is a living memory of Baruch.

We have started other traditions as well. When we have special events or family gatherings in our home, we light a candle in a special holder given to us by Baruch's aunt. During the holiday of Hanukkah, our tradition is that all the children have their own menorah to light. We have a miniature menorah we light for Baruch. On the menorah is written the word "Shalom." It means "hello," "good-bye," and "peace." We had only a few short hours to say hello and good-bye, but we know in our hearts he is at peace.

As if two pregnancy losses were not enough, in the winter of 1990 I had another early first trimester miscarriage. Finally, with much anticipation, we had a beautiful girl in March of 1991. And in October 1996 we welcomed to our family another beautiful daughter.

A LETTER TO OUR SON   *Estee and Howard Warsett*

We miss you on your birthday,
Each Rosh Hashanah.
This time of reflection
And family togetherness
Rekindles our dreams and hopes for you.
Such dreams and plans
Rich and beautiful,
Yet not to be fulfilled
For on this day God chose you
That you would be with Him.
Your innocence so divine.
Your soul so pure,
You need not be cleansed.
On the High Holy Day of Yom Kippur.
In the little time we had with you,
A great lesson we were taught —
How fragile life really is
And how quickly it is lost.
Each holiday we think of you
At this special family time.
You are entwined within our hearts.
And we'll never say goodbye.
We love you, Baruch, our forever baby.

Reprinted with permission of Fairview Press from *Remembering with Love* by Elizabeth Levang, Ph. D., and Sherokee Ilse. ©1992 by Elizabeth Levang and Sherokee Ilse.

PHYLLIS WAX lives in Milwaukee, Wisconsin, on a bluff over-looking Lake Michigan. Over the years she has been an active participant in a variety of political issues, including integration of schools and housing and, most recently, pre-serving abortion rights. She has been an editor, a bookstore proprietor, a gift shop and gallery manager, and a teacher.

Among the publications in which her work has appeared are *Wisconsin Academy Review, Plainsongs,* and *North Coast Review.* Her poetry was included in *Wisconsin Poets* at the Elvehjem Museum of Art and in two other anthologies: *When a Lifemate Dies* (Fairview Press) and *Other Testaments* (Incarnate Muse Publication). In April 1998, Phyllis was guest poet on Wisconsin Public Radio's "Hotel Milwaukee."

She writes:

"Tomorrow and Tomorrow and Tomorrow" was written in remembrance of my husband, Phil, who died of lung cancer at the age of 57. He was a lawyer and an accomplished pianist. He had a wonderful offbeat sense of humor. Holidays and fami-ly were very important to Phil, and he was an exuberant partici-pant in both. When Phil died, our younger daughter, Amy, had just started her senior year in college, and it is to her gradua-tion the poem refers. The first year is the hardest and the poem touches on events during that year which underlined his absence.

During his illness and after his death, I wrote poems about him and what was happening. Ten of these poems were printed in a small book which was given to family and friends at the dedication of his gravestone a year after he died. Our daugh-ters and others have mentioned re-rereading these poems from time to time.

TOMORROW, AND TOMORROW, AND TOMORROW

Phyllis Wax

Daughters, siblings, nephews, aunt,
we gather at the table
swallowing lumps
as someone else carves the turkey

Hugged by your jacket while I shovel the driveway,
I scatter salty drops which melt the ice

We lift our glasses for the kiddush
and start the Seder
straining to hear your voice

Look, I want to say,
a cardinal:
listen

Reprinted with permission of Fairview Press from *When a Lifemate Dies,* edited by Susan Heinlein, Grace Brumett, and Jane-Ellen Tibbals. ©1997 by Susan Heinlein, Grace Brumett, and Jane-Ellen Tibbals.

Flags fly on the greens
in Lake Park
but your clubs sit
cobwebbed in the garage

      A snatch of a Joplin rag,
      a phrase of Chopin,
      a soft suede cap,
      pizza, tapirs,
      songs around a campfire,

Herb's hospital room
    and I remember

      At commencement
      I must be proud
      enough for two

Each season I miss you
in a different way

R. W. SCHOLES   2 / 10 / 98

THANKSGIVING

GIVING THANKS
FOR THE TURKEY

Mary Logue

We watch mother stick
the thermometer in the turkey's
browned flesh and wonder: are we well?
are we getting better?

We once had a brother who threw
the black cat, Whiskers, up high
into the air to see the look of
alarm and limbs akimbo and we try
not to imagine how his body
must have flown across the freeway
hit by an unseeing car at sixty,
his legs and arms doing their last strokes
through the air. No place is set for
him at the dinner table. Dad watches
the football game alone.

We once had a sister who made up words
and drank too much, the words rising
out of her, the liquor taking their place,
little left in her when a stranger came
to steal her final breath away.

On this day we are subdues and spit
the thanks out of our mouths,
a splintered bone, dangerous to us,
wanting to lodge in our throats. We say
aloud, the pumpkin pie is good, the wild
rice is superb, and to ourselves, please,
let no one else be missing next year.

Let's start again. Let's give thanks for
ducks rising, lacy yarrow, window-paned ponds,
snow days, wood ticks, and glass jars full of agates.
Let's start at the other end of things,
where we see what has happened, where
the dog of understanding lies under
the table at our feet and waits for the turkey's neck.
We can begin by giving thanks for the turkey,
the bird of plenty, ugly and fierce in life,
comforting and delicious in death. We will
eat the light and dark meat of the turkey,
say, *it's done perfectly,* how could it be
any other way.

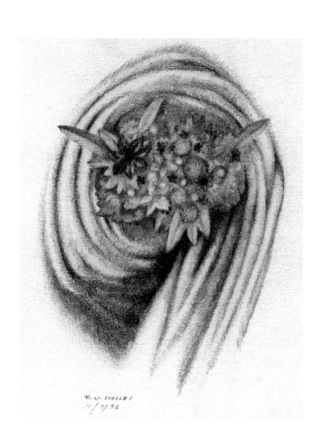

CHRISTMASTIME

NANCY WAMBACH is a teacher and writer living in San Jose, California. She is currently working on a collection of stories about a young widow, which will include "November."

About coping with holidays, she writes:

For me, anticipating the upcoming holiday—wondering how I could ever live through it—was always far more gut-wrenching than the actual experience. As a matter of fact, the day itself was often anticlimactic. I'd think afterwards, "Well, that wasn't so bad. Coulda been worse!"

What brings pain of the excruciating kind, where all you can do is clutch your chest and try to breathe, are the bolts from the blue, those completely unexpected memories and reminders that strike without warning: a familiar face, a song, a photo, a newspaper article. Milestones (marriages, graduations, friends' wedding anniversaries) can set you back, too.

My advice: the grief road is a long, arduous one, fraught with switchbacks and potholes. Be gentle with yourself. This is your own journey, although you never asked to take the ride, and you don't remember buying the ticket. Don't let others convince you to speed, no matter how uncomfortable your pain makes them. Let them wait: take as long as you need.

NOVEMBER

Nancy Wambach

DAVID WOULD HAVE wanted it this way. At least it seemed so at the time. Maybe I could preserve at least one tradition, show the kids we were still a family, only smaller now.

Every other Christmas since Peter and Nicole were toddlers, we'd driven to the mountain, slogged through the mud and needles, and chopped down our own tree.

On Thanksgiving morning, I awoke at 3:00 a.m., a regular occurrence since David's death. It had become my habit to lie there until dawn, concocting horrific scenarios regarding my fate and that of my fatherless children, now thirteen and eleven. This morning, however, I rose and began to stuff a twenty-pound turkey. I chopped celery and cried over onions to make my grandmother's special sausage dressing; I decorated myself with flour while blending in shortening for David's favorite pumpkin pie crust. Intermittently, when the nausea and fatigue that take residence in a grieving soul overtook me, I lay on the couch for a half hour or so. Then, with each new little burst of energy, I returned to the kitchen to peel potatoes and rutabagas, stir gravy, whip cream.

By 3:00 p.m., my face was flushed, my blouse was stained with the components of most of our menu, the table bore enough food for a Shriner's convention, and dinner was served. I hacked a few hunks off the turkey in the kitchen to avoid any awkward moments of realization that none of us had any idea how to carve.

We sat silent and grim, slicing and chewing dutifully, averting our eyes from the empty fourth chair. It seemed as good a time as any to broach the subject:

"What would you two think of going up on Sunday to get a tree?"

Nicole's fork made desultory swirls in her mashed potatoes. "Would we have to get up early? If we do, forget it."

Since her father's death six months earlier, she seemed to spend more hours each day asleep than awake. The circles under her eyes frightened me.

"No, not too early, hon. I just thought it would be nice, you know, something we could do together. What do you think, Peter?"

"I guess so, if you want to."

So it was settled. On a gray, drizzling Sunday morning after Thanksgiving, we piled into the family station wagon. I tested the windshield wipers to prepare for a torrent and couldn't help flinching a little at each assault of rain needles brailling the glass.

We started the long climb into the Santa Cruz Mountains. Nicole leaned against the door and stared out the window. Peter, upright and alert, watched for oncoming traffic, for any indication that the vulnerable family vehicle might be broadsided by a drunken maniac.

"Careful, Mom. Watch that guy on the right."

His fears about the wagon's frailty, at least, were probably groundless. It was a sturdy Ford, built and purchased in more optimistic days, and it rolled along the highway cradling its precious cargo, like a giant, surprisingly graceful beast. The steel-belted Michelin tires David had always insisted on carried it smoothly over bumps and ruts. ("Never, ever skimp where safety is concerned, honey. Remember that when you're on your own.")

I deliberately rested my tongue on my bottom lip to stop gritting my teeth.

"Uh, kids, does anyone remember how to get there?"

"Not me."

"Not me."

"There it is, Mom."

"No, I don't think so. It's further up."

"Wasn't it called Arrowhead Farms or something?"

"Loma Prieta, I think."

"That looks like it."

I'd always insisted that we return to the same farm year after year. Today they all looked identical to me, all peopled with happy, intact families.

Peter said, "Mom, I'm sure it was that one back there. I remember the little church across the street."

We pulled into a dirt driveway and emerged determined to complete our mission. We zipped up parkas and pulled gloves onto fingers already stiffening from the cold.

I'd always loved the scent of pine. Today it reminded me of the antiseptic cleaner used on the floor of David's hospital room.

"Your hat's in the box, Nicole."

"Oh, right, Mom. I'm really gonna wear a little kid's cap! Like that wouldn't be stupid beyond belief!"

"You always wear that cap, honey. You picked it out. You begged Daddy to buy it for you. Don't you remember?"

"How old was I? Six? Geez! That was like a million years ago! Anyway, my head's not cold. I'm not wearing it."

But she tucked the cap into her pocket anyway as she strode past me to catch up to her brother.

In stiff boots never worn more than once or twice a year, I tramped awkwardly through fudgy mud left by last night's rain.

A boy maybe sixteen years old squatted at the entrance, absently pulling sprigs of dead grass from the wet ground. He too sported a knit cap pulled over long, stringy hair; Peter nudged Nicole and whispered, "Hey, there's your twin. Dorky hat and all."

"Shut up, Buttface."

After grunting orders to cut only at the white line on any trunk, the seedy elf handed Peter a saw.

Rows and rows of trees and they all looked alike. Breathing hard, laboring to keep pace with my already-long-legged children, I began to doubt my memories of the not-so-distant past. Had I imagined it, that before my husband's illness, before the five years it took for him to die, I'd actually run two miles every day? Actually worried about cellulite and wrinkles? Did that really happen?

For a moment, I let my eyes linger upon the white line painted on each trunk. A whole forest of victims waiting to have their lives cut away just at the height of their beauty. They even made it easier for their murderers, directing, "Here! Cut here! Kill me here!"

It felt as if time had stopped for my little family.

In a couple of years, I'd actually be older than my husband ever would. If these present circumstances didn't kill me (a huge assumption, considering the way my heart lurched and kicked in my chest at times), perhaps someday I'd hold my grandchildren on my lap and show them the yellowed photos of a middle-aged man in outdated clothes and hairstyle.

I'd say, "This was your grandfather. I wish you could have known him. He would love you very much, as I do."

Maybe they'd play with the bulging veins on my wrinkled hands, stretch the folds of skin, look up at my white hair, at doting, filmy eyes, and try to imagine Grandma kissing this old-fashioned stranger.

"C'mon, Mom! We don't have forever!"

The children were now far ahead.

After a few cursory minutes of search and inspection, we agreed on a chubby fir with soft, tightly-clinging needles. Always before, I'd made a ceremony of encircling selected branches with my fingers and gliding them down the shaft—to check the tree for freshness.

At first, David balked at the logic of this. He'd say, "Honey, I can see how that might be important at a regular lot. After all, you don't know how long ago the tree was cut. But these are still growing! They're still alive. They have to be fresh!"

"I just like to do it. Am I hurting anyone?" I'd counter, and that would end it. I always had the final say about which tree we chose.

"Hey, Mom," Peter asked, "how tall is the living room ceiling?"

"I don't know. Why? You think the tree's too big?"

We stood on tiptoe next to it and tried to remember the height of the room. Why hadn't I thought of that before? Because David did.

We decided to risk it, and Peter set to work with the saw.

Nicole and I stood near, uncertain of our roles in this new circumstance, so we both touched the tree gingerly, in support.

Peter looked up, panting slightly from the unaccustomed exertion.

"Okay, Mom, about another quarter inch. Want to finish it?"

"Well, sure. All right." I'd never held a saw in my life before. But, by God, how hard could it be to slice a mere tree? I accepted the unwieldy, bow-like tool, with its arched wooden back and vicious steel points. In a determined frenzy, I pushed the saw back and forth against the solid trunk, feeling the teeth catch in the wood, watching the blade wobble.

Ping!

I straightened. "What the hell was that?"

"God, Mom, you broke the saw!" Nicole pressed her fingers to her forehead.

Peter sighed and shook his head in a mirror image of his father's familiar gesture.

"I knew it. I just knew it," I said to myself.

"Do I take a chance and let Mom use the saw, or do I just finish the job so we can get out of here?"

It seemed that, if I could just apply enough pressure on the little piece still gripping the trunk, I could separate it. I pushed my foot hard on the cut area. I tried to stand on it. Then I grabbed the top of the tree and tried to wrench it away. I ran in a slow, ungainly circle around the trunk, twisting the tree with me. I tried to cut some more, using just the maimed blade between two fingers. Finally I sliced an inch-long gash into my thumb.

"Goddamn son of a bitch!"

As I caught sight of my children's horrified faces, dizziness engulfed me again. I looked at the swinging broken blade, which by now resembled a fractured 1,000-year-old fossil of a shark's jaw, and carefully handed it to Nicole. Sliding down heavily on the muddy ground, I hugged my knees, lowered my head, and tried to take deep breaths. Droplets of blood stained my boot. I could smell sap bleeding from the tree.

People strode by, healthy saws in hand, inspecting with discriminating eyes the array of green merchandise. They gave wide birth to the row with the strange trio.

"C'mon, Mom, get up, okay? He was just being a butt," Nicole offered softly. She hissed at Peter, "Good one, idiot!"

Glaring at his sister, Peter said, "Look, Mom, it's no big deal. I'll just go ask the guy for another one. Try to get up, okay, Mom? C'mon. Please. People are looking."

He whispered to Nicole, "Take care of Mom. I'll be right back."

Nicole crouched beside me and inspected my finger.

"It's not too bad. You'll be okay."

She pulled the cap from her pocket.

"Here, hold this against it. He'll be back soon."

We sat in silence. Tentatively, she rubbed my arm.

Soon Peter arrived, triumphantly holding a new intact trophy aloft.

"I told him I broke it, Mom. He didn't even care. C'mon. Get up now. Okay?"

I wiped my nose on my sleeve and straightened my coat collar.

Clutching Nicole, I dragged myself up off the ground and wiped some mud off the seat of my pants. My finger wasn't bleeding much anymore.

Peter held out the new saw.

"Okay, Mom. Just put your hand on top of mine. We're gonna do this."

With two careful strokes, we sliced it clean and stood back as it softly, almost gracefully, fell. No snap or crash. What had been vibrant and healthy just minutes earlier now lay prone in the mud.

We dragged it to the pay booth and struggled together, ignored and unassisted by the entrance elf, to tie it to the car's roof with twine borrowed from the cashier.

Peter finally declared, "It'll hold as long as you take it easy, Mom. We can make it, I think. Let's go home."

That holiday season, the tree stood dark, heavy, and listing a bit to the right. Aside from opening gifts on Christmas morning, we rarely acknowledged its looming presence. We didn't show it off to friends who stopped by to see how the family was managing. Walking past the living room, I leveled my eyes forward and concentrated on my next step. But the three of us knew it was there. We'd put it there. And for that Christmas, the one we couldn't talk about for years, it would have to be enough.

THE BOX IN THE CLOSET: THOUGHTS ON MY DUE DATE
Carla J. Sofka

THERE IS A BOX IN THE CLOSET.

Inside the box, there is a tiny outfit made of snow-white cloth. Bright green threads stitched on the front proclaim a momentous occasion: Baby's First Christmas.

But there is so much more in that box in the closet.

It carries remnants of our hope, our plans, and anticipation of the holidays with our first baby. Our parents were eager to come to upstate New York in winter, the dread of snow and cold set aside to visit a new grandchild. We would laugh, smile, talk in silly voices, and make those funny faces that appear when a baby is in a room lit by Christmas lights.

The box carries my memories of preparation. I remember going to the baby section at a big department store during the end-of-winter sale. "You'll need these to keep the baby warm in winter," the clerk said. "You'll be glad that you bought them now—they'll be very expensive when you need them."

There were snowsuits for miniature people—material so soft and warm, and covered with bears, dinosaurs, balloons, and stars. "How much does a two-and-a-half-month-old baby weigh?" I asked. "What size will I need when the baby is that age?" I inquired. I wondered what it would be like to try to get my squirming baby into a snowsuit and zip it up.

Today I am reminded of that box in the closet.

This is the day that Jason or Carrie was supposed to be born.

Those brightly stitched threads still proclaim a momentous occasion—but one that won't happen this year.

Illogical but powerful thoughts overwhelm me: I should not have bought anything so early; if only I would have waited, the baby would be here. I must have jinxed my pregnancy by getting too excited. Why did I keep this Christmas outfit? A voice in my heart reminds me that I just could not take this one back.

This box makes me cry. I imagine a Christmas filled with emptiness, even though I will not be alone. There will be no toys around the Christmas tree. I will hang two stockings instead of three. I will hear holiday music, but I fear unbearable silence—a silence noticed only by me. There will not be coos, gurgles, hunger cries, or baby talk. Will there be laughter on Christmas Day?

There is a box in the closet filled with bittersweet memories of creating a life and experiencing a new life inside; it is also filled with the grief and pain of losing a baby.

There is a box in the closet that some day will be filled again with hope.

REVISITING THE BOX IN THE CLOSET

Carla J. Sofka

IT HAS BEEN ALMOST two-and-a-half years since I described the meaning of that box in the closet. While the box is still there, much has changed. Before describing how life is different, perhaps I should discuss something that may have made my experience a bit unique.

I make my living as an Assistant Professor in the Social Work Program at Skidmore College in Saratoga Springs, New York, where I specialize in research on grief and loss. In my earlier piece, I did not describe the significant effect my being a "death professional" had on me while experiencing a miscarriage. My teaching and scholarly responsibilities within academia clashed with my need to heal from my intense personal loss. I learned that the tenure clock which measures academic careers is not very sympathetic to the challenges I faced when my work was hitting too close to home.

I also discovered that knowledge may not always be helpful. While it was reassuring at times to know that my experiences were normal, the battles between my logical/cerebral self and my emotional self were often exhausting and unwelcome. I would catch myself wishing I didn't know anything about the way it was supposed to feel, so that it could just happen without all the anticipation. On the other hand, I discovered that some knowledge can be powerful. Perhaps it is the teacher in me that is compelled to write about that knowledge now.

Most grieving people are familiar with the "anniversary reaction," even if they do not know it by that name. It is the constellation of emotional, cognitive, and behavioral reactions that occur around a specific date or time of year that holds special meaning in relation to a significant loss in one's life. Pieces of my anniversary reaction were captured on October 4th, 1995, the due date for my first pregnancy, when I wrote "The Box in the Closet." The anticipated due date, the date of conception (if known), and the anniversary of the miscarriage itself are all days subject to the anniversary reaction. Many people have a similar reaction to holidays, because those times are often expected to be filled with joy and good cheer, a state of being that does not necessarily match the mood of someone who has experienced the loss of a child. Although it is helpful to know that this resurgence of grief is normal, the fact that I know in advance that these times are coming is often a curse.

My husband and I spent our first Christmas after the miscarriage with his father and family. I was relieved that we decided not to put up decorations at our house. I thought that this would help me to forget that there was a holiday coming up. Actually, things weren't too bad until the Christmas Eve service at my in-law's church. The people from the living nativity scene entered the church, and in "Mary's" arms was one of the youngest members of the congregation. Although the tears started to roll down my face during "Silent Night," I held myself together until the end of the service, and finally gave in to the tears and sobbing as we all walked to the car. I remember explaining the outburst away: "It's not that I'm not happy to be here [and this was true; my in-laws are great], it's that it's hard to be so far away from my parents on Christmas Eve. We went to the candlelight service together." I didn't give them the real reason for my tears because I wasn't sure that anyone would be able to understand. The topic of the miscarriage didn't seem to be on anyone's mind but my own.

After we got back to the house, I went upstairs and unpacked the heart-shaped candle that I had lit once before on October 4th. I had learned about the importance and comfort of ritual from my studies and my own experience, so I used this candle as something tangible, something that I could hold and keep to represent that which I lost. I watched the flame dance when my heart was heavy. Although there were no magic words that I could recite to take the pain away, it helped to have some quiet time to think about what might have been and to focus energy on healing my heart and body. I envisioned the light as rays of hope that would help my body get back on track, something that the doctor said should happen soon.

I also drew strength from taking part in a tradition that has largely faded into history, but one that can be revived by anyone who believes it will be useful. During the Victorian era, it was common to wear full mourning attire following the death of a loved one. Black clothing was a very effective way to nonverbally communicate that you are grieving. In the immediate aftermath of the loss, women would also wear special mourning jewelry that was also solid black. Sometimes they wore special broaches or rings that had a bit of the hair of the deceased woven into a pattern. The idea was to create a linking object, something with sentimental value or a personal item that had direct ties to the person who had died.

Obtaining such a linking object can be a challenge when you have had a miscarriage. If the miscarriage happened early in the pregnancy, there may not be anything tangible, not even an ultrasound photograph. In my case I had the hospital bracelet from my brief inpatient stay, but it just wasn't what I envisioned as something that I could hold on to. So, even though I hadn't yet regained all my strength, about a week after my surgery I decided to start looking for something that I could use to help focus on my grief and commemorate the tiny but important life that had only been a part of mine for six weeks. Off I went to the mall with hopes of finding a piece of jewelry that I could wear when I needed to remember.

In accordance with the tradition, I looked for something solid black. This was not an easy task. When sales people asked why it needed to be so specific, it was a bit tricky to decide whether or not to tell them. At moments when I felt like I could hold it together, I took the opportunity to teach them about mourning jewelry and several times was able to talk about my miscarriage. Some handled the information better than others. There were also times that I was only able to say that I needed to remember someone special, and they realized that it was probably best for both of us if there were no more questions.

I knew that I would recognize the right piece of jewelry when I saw it. Finally, in the very last store in the mall, I spotted the perfect piece. While it broke with tradition somewhat, the meaning and symbolism of the pin I chose came together in my heart and mind. It was a marcasite ring of small silver hearts encircling a single, dangling black onyx heart. To me the black heart represented the child I had lost; the silver hearts represented the hope for a child in the future, hope that I had to believe would eventually return.

I have worn the pin when I needed something tangible to remember the time that our baby was so strongly connected to my entire being, or when I needed something to help me cope with the lessons about loss that life was teaching me. People sometimes comment about the pin, and I carefully decide who gets a polite "thank you" and who might be able to handle the entire story.

I survived the first anniversary of the miscarriage and continued my visits with the doctor. After a year and a half of monthly and then bimonthly visits, being put on and taken off hormones, my body finally decided to cooperate. In September of 1996, the doctor said, "I don't need to see you for six months." Imagine his surprise when I returned in October and announced that I'd gotten a positive result on a home pregnancy test.

During the final week of September and the first week in October 1996, it seemed like I had simply gotten off one roller coaster ride and onto another. The juxtaposition of emotions as I approached the second anniversary of my original due date while waiting to confirm a subsequent pregnancy was overwhelming. While pangs of grief reminded me of what could happen, I couldn't squelch the building sense of excitement about possibly being pregnant again.

My doctor confirmed the pregnancy. He reassured me that he would do everything possible to help me cope with the fears that I expressed during that first prenatal visit. My husband Mike and I decided that we weren't going to tell anyone until we'd seen a heart beat on the ultrasound, and even then we weren't sure if it would feel right to tell our families. Those memories of difficult conversations informing them of the miscarriage were still quite strong.

At eight weeks, the heartbeat on the ultrasound made my heart dance with joy. However, as a former obstetric social worker who had seen too many heartbroken families, I knew all too well that I needed to remain a bit cautious. Thankfully, with a supportive doctor, who repeated an ultrasound at eighteen weeks, and great support from friends and family, I was able to let go of what I knew from my work and was able to enjoy a relatively uneventful pregnancy. On June 16th, my daughter Gwyndolyn Carrie was born.

The room with the box in the closet is now a nursery. In addition to that snow-white outfit, the box now contains Gwyn's red "Baby's First Christmas" outfit. The joys of being a parent and watching her change and grow are present every day. The remnants of grief reappear when they need to, and I use my candle lighting ritual and wear my jewelry during those times.

New challenges lie ahead. There may come a day when Gwyn will ask why she doesn't have a brother or sister. Will my knowledge on talking to kids about death be useful, or will I stutter until the emotions called up by the question subside? I'm not sure. If she's old enough, perhaps I'll take her to my jewelry box and show her the hospital bracelet and the circular pin, and explain to her their meaning. I'll also show her my new heart-shaped locket and explain that it expresses two distinct but intertwined meanings: half of the heart is subdued black onyx for my lingering sadness, and half of the heart has sparkling silver flowers for the joy that she brings to my life. Right now, I've got to remember that it's best not to expend too much energy worrying about it, for there is too much that I might miss in the meantime.

LYNN SCHULTZ: *I am a 47-year-old housewife, dairy farmer, and former school teacher. Having grown up on a small dairy farm, I developed a deep love for animals, the outdoors and the freedom of country living. A move to the city during my high school years led to college and degrees in Elementary Education and Health and Physical Education. While in college, I met my husband, who was also an education major with farming in his blood.*

We pursued both teaching and farming for a time, but, when our second son was about three, we decided one of us needed to quit teaching and tend the farm and the boys. We made improvements to our dairy farm, and I stayed home.

The delight of our lives came when our daughter Stacie was born in 1985. She grew to have the same love for animals and the outdoors as we did. Because she was with us so much, we tried to instill a sense of safety in her about the animals and equipment. But like all our children, she would beg for rides on the four-wheeler and tractor.

The evening of May 4, 1990, was warm and humid. When Dan finished filling a wagon with feed for cows, Stacie begged to ride the short distance from the silo to the feed lot. It was a short distance, so he gave in to her pleading and put her into the wagon. The wagon was specially designed to keep feed from falling out, so it seemed safe. But when Dan looked back, Stacie was not where he had put her. He stopped, but it was too late. The wagon had struck her in the head and neck. We performed CPR until the ambulance arrived. The ambulance personnel called a helicopter, but to no avail. The doctor said she had probably died immediately, and I guess, in my heart, I had known that all along.

There were other young people killed in our area around the time we lost Stacie. John Grandstrand, our funeral director, hired a grief support counselor, Mary Miller, to visit us and other bereaved people. This led to the Holiday Hope program, which focused on facing the holidays after a loss. Two and a half years after Stacie's death, Mary asked if I would speak to this gathering about coping with my loss and getting through the holidays. My piece in this book comes from my presentation that evening.

As the years have passed, we have reclaimed much of life's pleasantness, but I remember, many months after Stacie's death, longing for a time when we might not hurt so incredibly. I wondered if we would ever laugh spontaneously again, or regain the sense of humor that had been so much a part of our marriage and family. The support of a caring farm community and close relationships with several neighbors helped carry us through the many times when the going was difficult. Talking, crying, keeping active, and reading about grief helped us cope in the first year. But the stress took its toll. My husband suffered a heart attack, had to undergo bypass surgery, and developed a long-term case of depression. In addition, we lost a best friend in a car accident, and a 22-year-old nephew was killed in a fall from a ninth-story balcony while vacationing in Mexico. These setbacks have probably lengthened our journey.

After eight years, my husband says he has finally learned to deal with Stacie's death by not dealing with it. What he means is that he now understands that what happened cannot be changed. We both have found that dwelling on the terrible event kept us from feeling life again. The Serenity Prayer has truly hit home for us. When we give our pain over to God, or just let go of it, grief's grip is loosened.

STACIE

Lynn Schultz

ON MAY 4, 1990, my beautiful four-and-a-half-year-old daughter, Stacie, was killed in an accident on our farm. Though we always followed safety rules, my husband gave in that day when she pleaded to go with him. He put her in a feeder wagon that seemed impossible to get out of, but, as the saying goes, a moment of carelessness results in a lifetime of sorrow. Somehow she fell out, was hit by the wagon, and killed.

Stacie was our only girl and our youngest child. She was a delightful contrast to her older brothers, Aaron and Jason, who were then seventeen and twelve. Stacie was a vibrant, outgoing child, chatting easily with elderly women in the grocery store, introducing herself to other children everywhere we went so she "could play, too." She had an active and independent spirit, and she loved to please people. She was, as her gravestone says, "A very special child whose joyful spirit touched the hearts of many."

I tell you these things not so you will feel sorry for us, but so you can understand the bustle and excitement in our lives that was suddenly gone when she died, and why the transition has been so difficult. And when is the excitement of a child at its peak? During holidays, of course. When a child dies, special days like Christmas suddenly become a nightmare. When living day to day is a difficult task, how do you survive the holidays, or rather the "hellidays," as one friend has termed them?

Before I tell you how I have coped with Stacie's death, I must explain how my sense of grief and grieving has changed over time. You see, I have experienced several significant losses in my life. When my dad died eighteen years ago from a brain tumor, I grieved deeply, but, because he had been diagnosed with a terminal illness, I was prepared to some degree for his death, and relieved that his suffering was over. At that time, I was just starting my own family, so my eyes were turned more toward the future than the past. Still, the holidays were a time to gather together, share memories, and support family members.

Then just four and a half years ago, my husband's brother Larry died suddenly of a heart attack at the age of forty-three. We were very close, and the pain of losing him was intense. I realized that my husband and I were as fragile and mortal as Larry, and tomorrow no longer seemed so certain. More than ever, I saw the holidays as a time to draw together, to find and give support, to reminisce about the past, and to hold on to the present. It was hard for my sister-in-law to be there, we could tell. Still, we all wanted to help share her burden, and we were glad for any time we could spend together.

Then Stacie died, and everything was different. The pain was so overwhelming, I cannot put it into words. I faced that first holiday season with sheer terror. I began to dread its arrival as soon as I survived her birthday in August. I was like a wild animal: if something looked dangerous or threatening, I fled or avoided it. I had no control over the excruciating pain I felt, but I could control some of the situations that made it worse. Gathering together for the holidays meant pain multiplied, not eased. Now, I was the victim; I was the one who could not be consoled. Friends and family tried, and we were glad they did, but now I understood how my sister-in-law had felt when we gathered for holidays after Larry's death.

So how did I cope that first holiday season? In my search for ways to survive, my husband and I attended a hospice program designed to help the bereaved face the holidays. It was a lifesaver. Just seeing the other participants was helpful, because we knew we were not alone. We were offered lots of information and many helpful suggestions. Perhaps the most important realization we came away with was that, although things would never be the same, change was inevitable and we needed to accept it.

The changes to our holiday traditions were great. In the past, I had baked dozens of cookies and bars, and Stacie would help. Now I couldn't bring myself to bake anything. In the past, I had supervised the decorating of the tree, and Stacie would help. Now I knew I could not decorate a tree. I talked this over with my husband and boys, telling them they could do it if they wanted. As it turned out, no one felt like decorating, but twelve-year-old Jason did say, "Mom, you will be able to buy me some presents won't you?" I assured him I would. Also, because there was always an exchange of inexpensive gifts on both sides of the family, I felt I had to follow through with that.

I bought gifts with the help of a wonderful neighbor named Kathy. She called me in late November and said she was planning several short shopping trips into the city, and, if I wanted, she would take me and help with whatever was needed. I dreaded going to the store, so she was a godsend. I looked through newspapers and catalogs and made exact lists of what I needed for each person. When we got to the store, Kathy and I "power shopped," buying only what was on the list and then leaving. She was always considerate and understanding of my confusion and of my need to avoid certain areas. Shopping for short periods of time and not browsing for gifts made the task bearable.

The decision not to put up a Christmas tree bothered me. Stacie would really have missed a tree. Then one day near the end of November I realized what I could do. I went to a local tree farm and dug up a small pine tree, put it in a pot and took it to the cemetery. My husband, sons, and I strung popcorn and cranberries and hung several of Stacie's favorite ornaments on it. The rest of my family asked if they could add things, and I said yes, so each time I visited it, there was another special item that someone had added. It gave all of us a chance to give Stacie one more gift. I have gotten a new tree each year since, and in the spring I plant the tree in our yard. How long will this continue? I cannot say, but it seems the right thing for now.

Another suggestion we took from the hospice was to let relatives know well in advance what we could and could not handle. I knew I could not bear Christmas at my in-laws. My brother-in-law always dressed up as Santa and passed out gifts to the young children. Stacie had hung by his side the year before. I could not face that situation. Their laughter and hugs would have torn my broken heart out. Another problem was that they lived one hundred twenty miles away, so it meant staying overnight. I would have felt trapped, unable to flee to the safety of my home. I told them in early November that I was sure I could not be there. They were disappointed but understood. My husband and the boys did go and handled the gathering okay. I was glad for them.

I did attend the gathering that was held for my side of the family. There was not the excitement of small children to deal with. Even so, the calm and quiet was hard to deal with in its own way. We joined the gathering for mealtime. I prepared no food, which was another change from the past. We exchanged gifts, with Jason passing them out. Then my husband and I headed home. I was glad to have the routine of doing chores to finish passing the day. We let the boys stay with their cousins so they did not feel cheated out of Christmas Eve tradition.

We survived the first holiday season. At some point, some caring people sent a Christmas centerpiece and a poinsettia plant, so we did have holiday color after all. The second Christmas was not quite as painful, but still nothing like Christmas had been before Stacie's death. Again, I avoided buying a tree, but I did hang a new string of cow-shaped lights I had bought, and I put out some candles. I went to Christmas at my in-laws. It hurt tremendously, but I spent the difficult times in another room, ignoring the festivities. I honestly do not know what this year will bring. We have been so busy with the late harvest on the farm that I have not had much chance to think about the holiday. That tells me I must be healing.

It has been difficult to balance my needs with the needs of others during the holidays. I know it has not been easy for our families, but they have been understanding, and most importantly, they have not been judgmental.

The hustle and bustle and excitement of past holidays has been replaced by a quiet acknowledgment of their true meaning for us, that God's son was born so he could die for us. I take comfort from knowing that God understands how I feel.

We've been surrounded by caring people who are not afraid of us, as can sometimes happen. We have sought out others who understand our grief. I have read and re-read many books on coping with my loss. I have begun the healing process, but a part of me has been cut away and I will bleed forevermore.

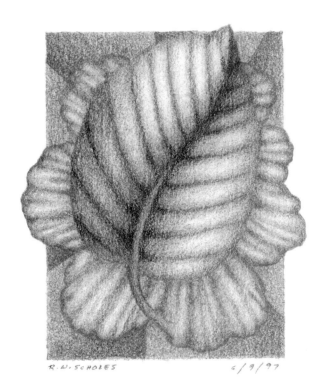

R. N. SCHOLES   6/9/97

Other Grief and Bereavement Resources
from Fairview Press

Cry Until You Laugh: Comforting Guidance for Coping with Grief by Richard J. Obershaw, MSW, LICSW. ISBN 1-57749-063-0, paperback, 6 x 9, 192 pages, $12.95. Down-to-earth advice that interjects gentle humor into a painful topic.

Help Me Say Goodbye: Activities for Helping Kids Cope When a Special Person Dies by Janis Silverman, M.A. ISBN 1-57749-085-1, paperback, 10 x 7, 32 pages, $6.95. An art therapy and activity book for children coping with the death of someone they love.

When Men Grieve: Why Men Grieve Differently and How You Can Help by Elizabeth Levang, Ph.D. ISBN 1-57749-078-9, paperback, 6 x 9, 192 pages, $14.95. A unique resource for grieving men and those who love them.

Our Stories of Miscarriage: Healing with Words edited by Rachel Faldet and Karen Fitton. ISBN 1-57749-033-9, paperback, 6 x 9, 224 pages, $13.95. Fifty contributors, including four men, share vivid accounts of how miscarriage changed their lives.

Remembering with Love: Messages of Hope for the First Year of Grieving and Beyond by Elizabeth Levang, Ph.D., and Sherokee Ilse. ISBN 0-925190-86-1, paperback, 4½ x 7½, 320 pages, $11.95. Daily readings and affirmations for the first year after a loss, and beyond.

When a Lifemate Dies: Stories of Love, Loss, and Healing edited by Susan Heinlein, Grace Brumett, and Jane-Ellen Tibbals. ISBN 1-57749-056-8, paperback, 6 x 9, 256 pages, $14.95. A moving collection of stories, poems, essays, and journal entries that recount the real experiences of people who have had to deal with the loss of a lifemate.

To order, call toll-free 1-800-544-8207.